Where to go
Bird Watching in Canada

Where to go

Bird Watching in Canada

by
David Stirling and
Jim Woodford

Hancock House Publishers

ISBN 0-919654-28-2

Printed in Canada
Second Printing 1976

Published by

hancock

house

HANCOCK HOUSE PUBLISHERS LTD.
3215 Island View Road,
Saanichton, B.C., Canada.

CONTENTS 🌿🌿🌿

BIRDING IN THE
ATLANTIC PROVINCES

INTRODUCTION

David Stirling

Birdwatching has long been a popular outdoor activity. Of the thousands of people interested in natural history, birdwatchers, or birders, are by far the most active and enthusiastic. In fact, many natural history societies evolved from bird clubs and most of their active members are birders. Unlike most other branches of natural history birdwatching is the domain of the enthusiastic and knowledgeable amateur.

Birdwatching and bird finding are almost synonymous terms. The travelling birder wants to know "which birds are where at what time". This information may be difficult for a visitor to a new area to acquire, unless he has local assistance. From the accumulated knowledge of many birders have come articles and books devoted to bird finding.

Knowing habitats is very important in finding birds. Each habitat has its own species and the knowledgeable birder must also be an ecologist. Sometimes the last refuge of a species may be a small piece of its unique habitat surrounded by a landscape completely altered by man. Knowing the special requirements of the Black Oyster Catcher or the White-eyed Vireo can lead the birdwatcher to these species but if the exact locations are available in print it is even easier.

The season is another important factor in bird finding. The boreal forest alive with warblers and other species in June is almost birdless in December;

the prairie marsh, a veritable bird city in summer, becomes a frozen wasteland of snow and broken reeds in winter. The opposite may be true for other habitats. The west coast bay, devoid of birds in July, may be thronged with waterfowl in January. In migration times, usually spring and fall, spectacular numbers of birds may congregate in a particular place or pass over a certain area.

The birder armed with his binoculars, checklist and this guide can look forward to many pleasant hours in the field from the Bay of Fundy to the Strait of Georgia.

Good luck in your bird finding!

BALD EAGLE   David Hancock

BIRD WATCHING 🪶🪶🪶

Bird watching is a disease. It can strike quickly and without regard to age or sex. According to recent surveys there are over 12,000,000 birdwatchers in North America — truly a disease of epidemic proportions. But why? The answer is simple. Birds are everywhere from the back yard to wilderness areas of every continent.

Their diversity of size, shape, color and behavior offer exciting challenges for indoor or outdoor recreation. Birdwatching can be a private interlude in the day, a social gathering, a science or a business through the sale of your stories or photographs of birds.

In fact, bird watching is big business. More books are devoted to the birds than any other field of natural history. Hundreds of millions of dollars are spent annually on automobiles, motels and travel tours directly by people pursuing birds. Cameras, binoculars, telescopes and tape recorder sales to birders contribute even more. And the manufacture of bird feeders and sale of bird food supports thousands of persons.

Good binoculars and an easy to use field guide are the essential tools for the birdwatcher. However, disease can cause fever and irrational behaviour and this I suspect is the reason so many birders tumble into the woods armed with extra check lists, cameras and a multiple of lenses, and tape recorders with parabolic reflectors. The following is a brief introduction to the hardware of birdwatching.

COMMON PUFFIN   S. Kress

FIELD GUIDES

A good field guide contains clear illustrations of the birds for easy identification, a range map to quickly tell when and where the bird is likely to be, and a brief description of the bird's behaviour, habitat, and easily identifiable characteristics. Nothing more need to be said than GET:

Birds of North America by Robbins, Bruun, Zim and Singer. Golden Press. Hard or soft bound.

Or the slightly less efficient and more costly two volume series: Field Guide to the Birds of Eastern N.A. and Field Guide to the Birds of Western N.A. by R. T. Peterson, Houghton Mifflin Co.

CANADA GEESE   Tom W. Hall

BIRD CHECK LISTS 🪶

Check lists are simply a local (city) or regional com-
pilation of all birds found in the area concerned (see
page 110). They are made of stiff card for carrying in
the pocket or field guide. They usually state whether
a bird is commonly or rarely seen and at what season.
Most Natural History Clubs make these available to
visiting birders free of charge or 10 to 15 cents each.
They make it easy to record the day's sightings and
form a permanent record. Get them for the areas you
visit.

BALD EAGLE   David Hancock

14

CANADA GEESE   Tom W. Hall

BINOCULARS

These come in a wide range of quality, price and power. Don't get a magnification of more than 6, 7, or 8 power. It's impossible to hold more powerful ones steady under perfect conditions, let alone after running 100 yards through the woods after a 'new bird'. For the untried beginner many excellent, yet heavier weight pairs, can be purchased for 20 to 50 dollars. Avoid the 200 to 300 dollar pairs. Recent advances in optics and light-weight bodies such as the Nikon ultra-compact prism binoculars bring quality, durability and light weight for 60 to 90 dollars. The above come in a magnification of 6, 7 or 8.

Scopes are a specialist's tools, requiring more investment and a good tripod to mount them on. Forget this implement until your binoculars are well used.

PHOTOGRAPHY

Without proper care bird photography can become the most malignant outgrowth of birding, draining dollars, time and the spouse's patience. On the other hand, the ultimate challenge to seeing a new bird or exciting behavior is to record it on film for later reference, or for friends, business or science. The photographs of this book come almost exclusively from amateur birder-naturalists. And why not make an enjoyable hobby pay its way?

There are two important features in bird photography. First, you must know the habits of your subjects. That is, know where to go and to look for them; to be able to predict their behavior patterns and to understand their tolerances to your disturbance. Once you have found out where a bird is likely to appear, then only patient waiting (often from the seclusion of a blind) is required to capture exciting moments on film. That is, provided you thoroughly understand the second important feature of photography — the operation of your camera and film. There are dozens of good camera makes and models highly suitable for bird photography. Unfortunately, many camera stores give advice dependent upon the availability of stock and the discount that they make on selling. Below are some general and specific recommendations that suit this photographer. First, get a reflex camera — where you look through the lens to see exactly what is being photographed and whether it is in focus. Second, the 35mm format is most flexible for optional lenses and attachments, is light-weight to carry, is simple and quick to use, and

PIED-BILLED GREBES   Eric Hosking

is economical to keep fed with film. Two basic lenses
will take 99 percent of your pictures. First is a Macro
lens with a nearly normal focal length 50-55mm. The
macro lens permits pictures to be taken within one
foot. This is particularly important if you are out
birding and want a close-up of a bee, flower or nest.
Oh, you're not interested in insects and flowers? Well,
the birds are and most birders quickly develop an ap-
preciation of all nature. The second lens I recommend you get in a telephoto of moderate length —
150 to 200 mm. This can be hand held at 125th of a
second to give flexibility for 'opportunistic' photography. That is, getting a picture whenever you can.
This is opposed to setting up the equipment in a
blind, possibly with strobe lights and a super abun-

RUBY-THROATED HUMMINGBIRD   W. Goodpaster

dance of patience. A large telephoto of 400 to 500mm is a seldom used frill that can come much, much, later.

In wildlife photography it is often desirable to change lenses quickly to get a shot of a fleeting subject. Here a bayonet mount on the lens is helpful. Also, go the few extra dollars and get a through-the-lens meter or even a fully automatic camera. This eliminates worrying about a separate meter getting wet, banged or lost, or of remembering to take it with you or use it.

The through-the-lens meter is always there and its one or two faults are more easily corrected than in a separate meter. The camera manufacturer will outline another 101 features of his product, but most are quite insignificant to general or bird photography. Here we are speaking of a camera and lens in the 300 or 400 dollar range. This is a minimum outlay for new equipment though the same second hand items can be acquired for one third to one half price. In fact, 500 dollars will give you a new outfit with the two lenses. The accommodating shop clerk will be pleased to throw in a free roll of film knowing he has another birder hooked. The new Minolta or Pentax 35mm camera wraps up all the above features with durability and lightness of weight — again an important consideration. By the time you have tramped 10 hours with your left pocket bulging with field guide, check list and a few chocolate bars; the right pocket full of film and an extra lens; your binoculars around your neck; the camera over your shoulder or mounted on a tripod across your shoulder, you are conscious of each extra ounce. When at the last moment you decide to leave the lunch at home in order to carry an extra lens you know you are thoroughly initiated as a bird-photographer — a hungry but happy one.

SOUND RECORDING

Recording bird song was a specialist's hobby and has become popular and practical by the development of high quality Cassette Recorders for under 100 dollars. A birder in Toronto, Canada, Dan Gibson, has developed a portable reflector which weighs less than three and a half pounds and has a frequency response to 15,000 cycles. It is now feasible for the weekend naturalist to record professional quality wildlife sound to elaborate his slide talks or sound his movies. Movies! ! Oh, oh, I had hoped to avoid mentioning that category. Learn well 35mm still photography before you even consider movies. The quality of 8mm movies is simply too disappointing for the effort.

Super 8 is better, but once bitten by the bug you won't be satisfied until you have 16mm. The camera and lenses will begin at 1200 dollars. Add a good tripod — the key to good movies — and you set out another 500 dollars — yes, 500 dollars for the tripod alone. And film — if you only shoot four times the amount of film that ends up in your final production, and that is a very good ratio for wildlife footage, you will have about 20 dollars worth of film per viewing minute — that's 1200 dollars per hour. But this cheap method means running the original film through a projector where it's going to get scratched and no longer saleable. That's taboo. So you have a copy made before you even view the processed film — another 600 to 800 dollars, please. Then you add . . . please start your photography with 35mm slides, then if your banker is friendly, think of movies.

ROBIN   Tom W. Hall

BALD EAGLE   David Hancock

BIRDING IN
BRITISH COLUMBIA 🍃🍃🍃

British Columbia is a land of contrasts. Bordered on the south by the 49th parallel; on the north by the 60th; on the east by the towering Rocky Mountains and the 120th Meridian, and on the west by the open Pacific Ocean, British Columbian encloses 355,855 square miles. In the southern part of a succession of major mountain ranges and valleys runs north and south. The topography and the prevailing winds from the Pacific Ocean create a series of wet and dry regions between the coast and the Rockies. Western mountain slopes are usually wet and heavily wooded, while eastern slopes are dry — sometimes almost arid — and more open. Ranges in the northern part of the province generally lower, forming extensive plateaus. Here the wet and dry areas, so marked in the south, are not nearly so pronounced. Cold, dry Polar Continental air pours down from the Arctic across this corrugated battlefield to further modify the wet and dry patterns. Nowhere else in Canada does such diversity of habitats for animals occur.

Over ninety-five per cent of the bird species found in Canada have been recorded in British Columbia, reflecting this diversity.

Man not only classifies and names individual plants and animals, but he also tries to categorize the different associations of plants and animals into 'Biotic Areas'. These are primarily characterized by the species of plants found there. The kinds of plants are determined by the climate, which is in turn a product of latitude, altitude, and prevailing winds.

Birds, because of their mobility, do not fit so well into Biotic Areas. Certain kinds range far and wide. Others, much more specialized, are found only in specific places. This may appear contradictory, but then birds are contradictory creatures.

COMMON MURRES   David Hancock

WESTERN WOOD PEWEE   Kathleen Morck

Within the Biotic Areas are many habitat niches, the actual area lived in by a species. In each niche, the micro-climate and vegetation inhabited by the birds is different from that in adjacent niches. A good bird-watcher 'plays' his habitats. That is, he knows what to expect in any particular area. For instance, the birds you would expect to find in farming country habitat are quite different from those you would find in a forest habitat in the same broad biotic zone. In the riparian woodlands of the Dry Forest Biotic Area you will find many species, including the Black-headed Grosbeak, Bullock's Oriole, Redstart, Red-eyed Vireo, Catbird and Veery. Coniferous and boreal forests generally have fewer birds because even-age stands of one tree species provide fewer niches. Forest fires, by wiping out the coniferous trees and allowing light to penetrate to the ground, help to produce a new habitat of deciduous trees and annual plants. This altered habitat contains a greater diversity of niches, and therefore has many more bird species than the surrounding dark forests.

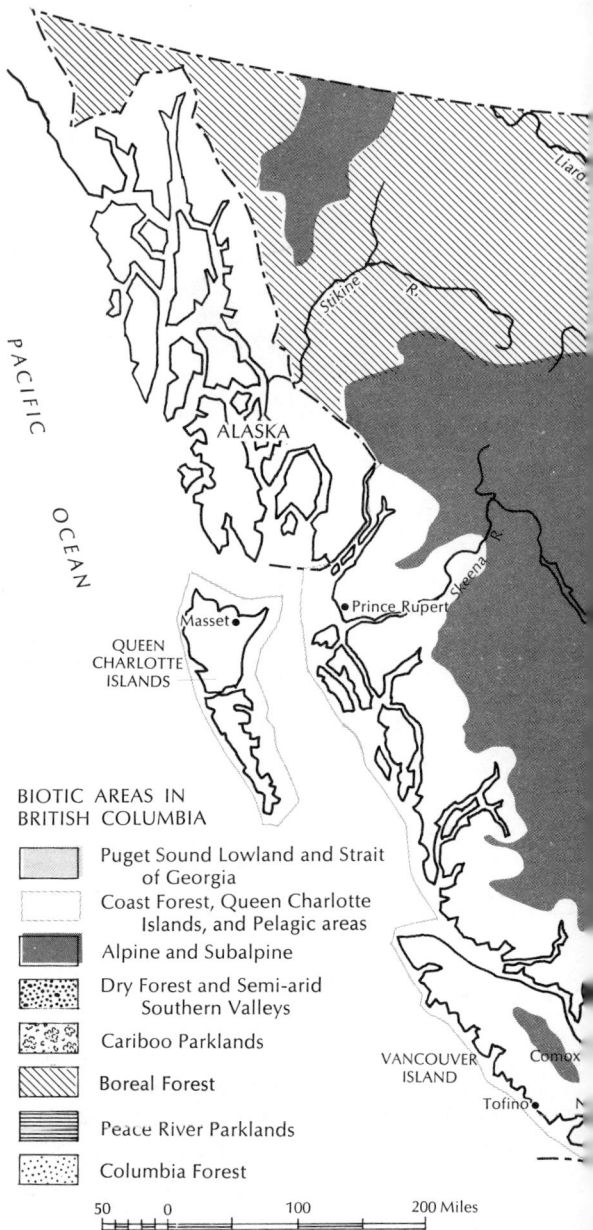

PACIFIC

OCEAN

Liard

Stikine R.

Skeena R.

ALASKA

• Prince Rupert

Masset •

QUEEN
CHARLOTTE
ISLANDS

BIOTIC AREAS IN
BRITISH COLUMBIA

	Puget Sound Lowland and Strait of Georgia
	Coast Forest, Queen Charlotte Islands, and Pelagic areas
	Alpine and Subalpine
	Dry Forest and Semi-arid Southern Valleys
	Cariboo Parklands
	Boreal Forest
	Peace River Parklands
	Columbia Forest

VANCOUVER
ISLAND

Comox

Tofino •

50   0   100   200 Miles

BRITISH COLUMBIA
BIOTIC AREAS

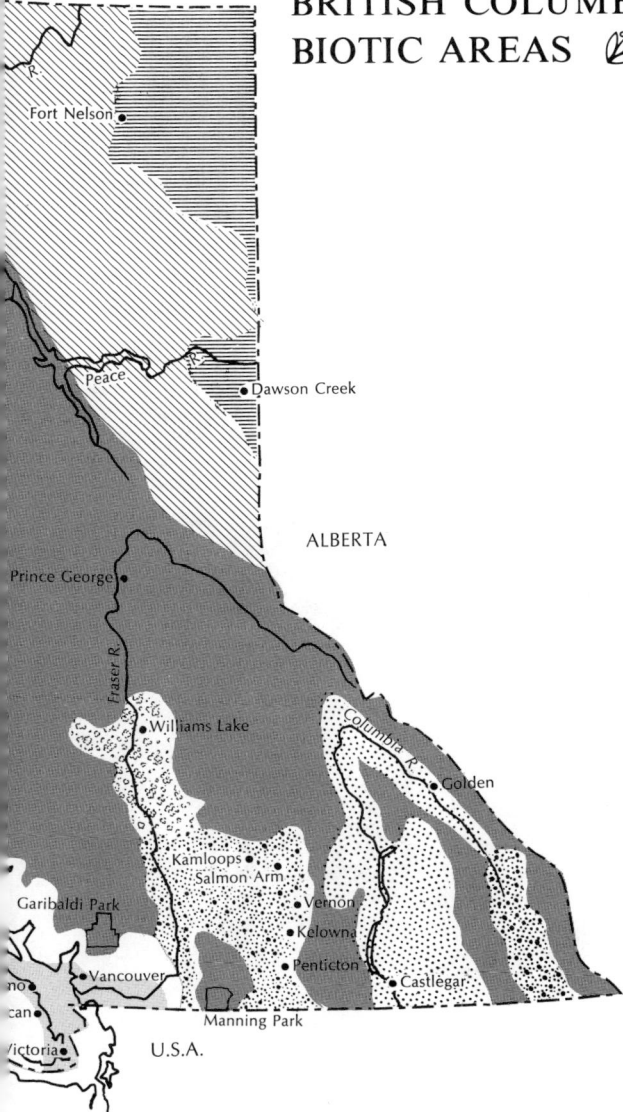

R.

Fort Nelson

Peace

Dawson Creek

ALBERTA

Prince George

Fraser R.

Williams Lake

Columbia R.

Golden

Kamloops
Salmon Arm

Vernon

Garibaldi Park

Kelown

Penticton

Castlegar

Vancouver

Manning Park

can

Victoria

U.S.A.

PUGET SOUND LOWLAND: STRAITS OF GEORGIA 🦅

This is Canada's most favored place for man and birds, with mild winters, cool sunny summers and low rainfall. The vegetation is an association of Douglas-fir, arbutus and Garry oak, though the two latter species are missing in the Fraser Valley. More than two-thirds of the province's human population and bird species are found here.

DOUBLE-CRESTED CORMORANTS   David Hancock

VICTORIA AREA

Clover Point: The sewer outlet on Dallas Road is a prime area for gulls, ducks, grebes, loons, shorebirds, rare pelagic species and birdwatchers. The whole waterfront area makes a good birding drive. Best times — August to May.

Esquimalt Lagoon: Cormorants, loons, grebes, ducks, gulls, terns and jaegers. Bald Eagles nest behind the lagoon, other pairs nest at Elk Lake and on Discovery Island off Oak Bay. Best time — October to May.

Central Saanich — Island View Beach: All four species of loons have been seen at Island View Beach. Rhinoceros Auklets and Heermann's Gulls are common in summer. The area is known for its wintering waterfowl, skylarks, and as a good place for the rarer raptors such as Roughleg Hawk, Peregrine and Gyr Falcons. Best times — late fall and winter.

OYSTERCATCHERS   David Hancock

Goldstream Provincial Park: A good place to see Dippers, Steller's Jays and Varied Thrush. The annual Chum salmon spawn in October and November concentrates birds and people.

Active Pass: (On the ferry route from Vancouver to Victoria). Huge flocks of Brandt's Cormorants, Arctic Loons, Bonaparte's Gulls (late April and early May), and 10-50 Bald Eagles are common here. Seven pairs of eagles nest in the pass. Best time — October to June. See Hancock Ferry Guide to Vancouver Island for nest locations etc.

Mittlenatch Island Nature Park: Organized excursions to bird rookery leave from Miracle Beach daily during July and August. Nesting colonies of Glaucous-winged Gulls, Pelagic Cormorants, Black Oystercatchers and Pigeon Guillemots are visited.

VANCOUVER AREA

Reifel Waterfowl Refuge: This area hosts Canada's largest wintering concentrations of waterfowl, including 40,000 Snow Geese. The refuge also has a large display of captive waterfowl of the world. It is an excellent area for birds of prey, including Peregrine Falcon and Snowy Owls. Best times — September to May.

Iona Island: Excellent for grebes, ducks, many hawks and owls, small passerines. Best times — September to May.

Pitt Meadows: Green Herons, ducks, Sandhill Cranes, gulls, wintering hawks and owls. Best time — all year.

Stanley Park: Excellent for sea birds, waterfowl, nesting Bald Eagles, coast forest passerines. Best time — all year.

STELLER'S BLUE JAY   Tom Willock

COAST FOREST,
QUEEN CHARLOTTE ISLANDS
and PELAGIC 🐦

Coast Forest, Queen Charlotte Island and Pelagic:
(Tofino, Prince Rupert, Masset). This extensive area
of western British Columbia has mild winters, cool
summers and heavy rainfall — 50-200 inches. The
vegetation comprises heavy forests of western hemlock, amabilis fir, Douglas fir or sitka spruce. A
dense understory of salmon berry and salal occurs
where light reaches the ground. Characteristic birds:

OLD SQUAW DUCK

TUFTED PUFFIN

RHINOCEROS AUKLET   David Hancock

Red-breasted Sapsucker, Steller's Jay, Chestnut-backed Chickadee, Varied Thrush, Bald Eagle (along shore), Townsend's Warbler (summer). Some of the most colorful and unusual birds of North America are found on the isolated offshore islands. They include the Tufted Puffin, Common Murres, murrelets, Rhinoceros Auklets and petrels. The Queen Charlotte Islands still have a good breeding population of Peregrine Falcons. The offshore waters have shearwaters, Black-footed Albatross, Fulmars, kittiwakes and Sabine's Gulls. Pelagic birding trips are regular features in May and September from Tofino, Vancouver Island and Westport, Washington.

PEREGRINE FALCON   David Hancock

ALPINE & SUB-ALPINE

Alpine and Sub-alpine: These regions cover a vast area of British Columbia. Here there are long, cold winters and short, cool summers of 2-3 months. The sub-alpine area has alpine fir, mountain hemlock and Engleman's spruce. The alpine area has flower meadows, bare rock and ice. Most of these regions

WHITE-TAILED PTARMIGAN IN SUMMER PLUMAGE

are inaccessible to the average birdwatcher, though recently ski development and logging access roads have opened up some mountain tops. Both Manning Park and Garibaldi Park offer excellent opportunities to examine these biotic types. Characteristic birds above timberline are White-tailed Ptarmigan and Gray-crowned Rosy Finch. At timberline Clark's Nut-cracker, Fox Sparrow and Golden-crowned Sparrow are found. Best times — July to September.

WHITE-TAILED PTARMIGAN   Tom W. Hall

DRY FOREST & SEMI-ARID SOUTHERN VALLEYS 🖋

Dry Forest and Semi-arid Southern Valleys: (Kamloops, Kelowna, Penticton). Here mild winters and long, hot summers again create favored living conditions for man and birds, though summer visitors are most abundant. Low valleys have bunch grass and sage brush, much of which has been lost to orchards and towns. Slopes and hills have yellow pine and Douglas-fir. Stream margins have thick deciduous growth of aspen, cotton-woods, birch, choke cherry, Saskatoon berry and willows. Characteristic birds are Rock Wren, White-breasted Nuthatch, White-throated Swift (Vaseux Lake), Catbird, Western Kingbird, Say's Phoebe, Lazuli Bunting, Bullock's Oriole, Poorwill and Yellow breasted Chat. Rarer species are the White-headed Woodpecker, Williamson's Sapsucker (Western larch forests), Sage Thrasher and Prairie Falcon.

SHARP-TAILED GROUSE   Kathleen Morck

PRAIRIE FALCON   Tom Willock

TRUMPETER SWANS   David Hancock

37

CARIBOO PARKLAND 🦜

Cariboo Parkland: (Williams Lake, Prince George). Cold winters, short warm summers, and light precipitation are characteristic of this area. Many lakes, sloughs and meadows punctuate the flat and rolling lands which are forested with lodgepole pine, aspen and Douglas-fir. Cariboo sloughs are much like those of the prairies. Here we have an abundance of nesting and Yellow-headed Blackbirds. The only known nesting area for the White Pelican in British Columbia is located in this region at Stum Lake. The uplands have Yellow-bellied Sapsuckers, Mountain Bluebirds, Olive-sided Flycatchers, Tree Swallows and Townsend's Solitaires. Best time — May to October.

WHIMBREL   Eric Hosking

WHITE-WINGED SCOTER   David Hancock

BOREAL FOREST 🦅

Boreal Forest (Fort Nelson). This area in northern and north-eastern British Columbia has cold long winters, and short cool summers. White spruce, black spruce, tamarack, aspen and black cottonwood are the common trees. Birds here are mostly summer residents and low in number. They include the Hermit Thrush, Yellow-bellied Sapsuckers, Yellow-bellied Flycatcher, Black-poll Warbler and Slate-colored Junco. Resident species include Spruce Grouse, Gray Jay, Raven, Three-toed Woodpeckers and Pine Grosbeak.

BLACK-BILLED MAGPIES   Tom Willock

PEACE RIVER PARKLAND 🦅

Peace River Parkland: (Dawson Creek). This area in north-eastern British Columbia is an extension of the Prairie Provinces' Parklands. It has more deciduous woodland and open places than the boreal forest. Winters are cold, summers warm and the precipitation is moderate. Several bird species characteristic of north-eastern North America enter the province here. To be expected are Baltimore Oriole, Blue Jay, Rose-breasted Grosbeak, Sharp-tailed Grouse, Common Grackle. The Snowy Owl is a regular winter visitor but breeds only in the Arctic.

COLUMBIA FOREST 🍃

Columbia Forest: (Castlegar, Golden). This is the type of forest found at low elevations in the Kootenay and Arrow Lakes regions and along the Columbia River. Winters are moderately cold, summers are hot, and precipitation is heavy year round. Trees of this area are similar to those of the coast: western red cedar, western hemlock and grand fir, plus western larch and white birch. The bird fauna, too, is much like that of the coast and includes Steller's Jay, Varied Thrush, Dipper, Black Swift and Chestnut-backed Chickadee (the true coniferous forest chickadee).

CLIFF SWALLOWS   Tom Willock

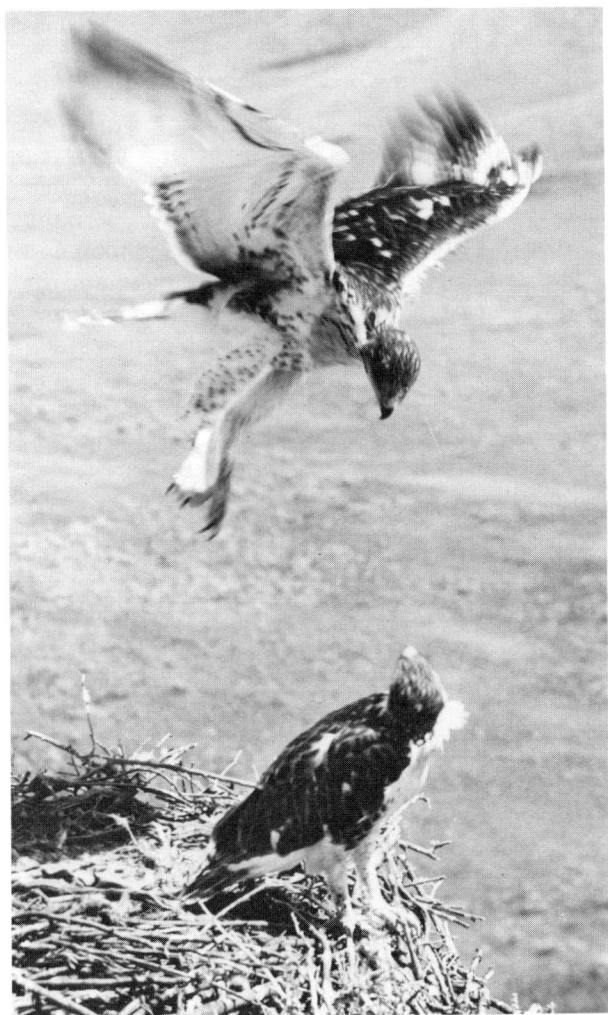

FERRUGINOUS HAWK   Tom Willock

BIRDING IN ALBERTA, SASKATCHEWAN AND MANITOBA ✸✸✸

Tempting as it is for outsiders to refer to Alberta, Saskatchewan and Manitoba as the Prairie Provinces and conjur up visions of featureless plains of wheat or frozen expanses of drifting snow, these three provinces cover as much diversity of habitats as any major geographical division of Canada. The main barriers that restrict human activities within and to the southern half or one third of these provinces also play a major role in the distribution of birds.

The great upward thrust of the Rocky Mountains restricts westward movement and directs bird migration and dispersal in a northsouth direction. The variability of habitats from tundra dwelling White-tailed Ptarmigan to the cone eating Red Crossbills.

The second division, the Great Plains proper, extends from the Texas Gulf Coast to the mouth of the Mackenzie River, and certainly constitutes the major feature of the provinces. Biologically the plains are broken up into three major regions. The Prairies in the south are characterized by the harshest climate and the best soil. Rainfall is low and unreliable and it is little wonder that the bird life is primarily associated with the pothole lakes and sloughs. Muddy, and rich in insects, aquatic plants, molluscs, crustaceans, and amphibians, the ponds support innumerable ducks, loons, grebes, herons, terns, swans and geese. Wascana Bird Sanctuary, 360 acres of manmade

ALBERTA, SASKATCHEWAN & MANITOBA 🌿

KEY TO LIFE ZONES
FOR MAP OF
ALBERTA, SASKATCHEWAN
AND MANITOBA

■ Rocky Mountains

Great Plains—

▨ Boreal Forest

▨ Parkland

▤ Prairie

▥ Canadian Shield

0   100   200 Miles

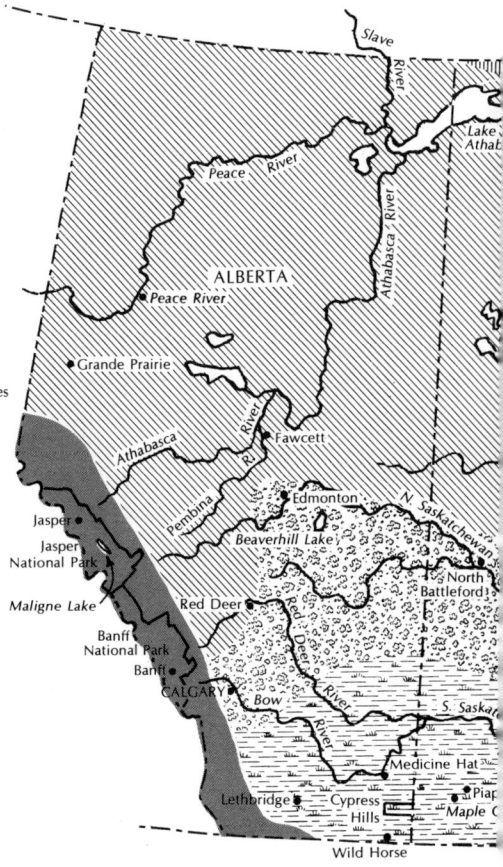

Slave River

Lake Athab.

Peace River

ALBERTA

Peace River

Grande Prairie

Athabasca River

Fawcett

Pembina River

Jasper

Jasper National Park

Edmonton

Beaverhill Lake

N. Saskatchewan River

Maligne Lake

Red Deer

North Battleford

Banff National Park

Banff

Red Deer River

CALGARY

Bow River

S. Saska.

Medicine Hat

Lethbridge

Cypress Hills

Piap

Maple C.

Wild Horse

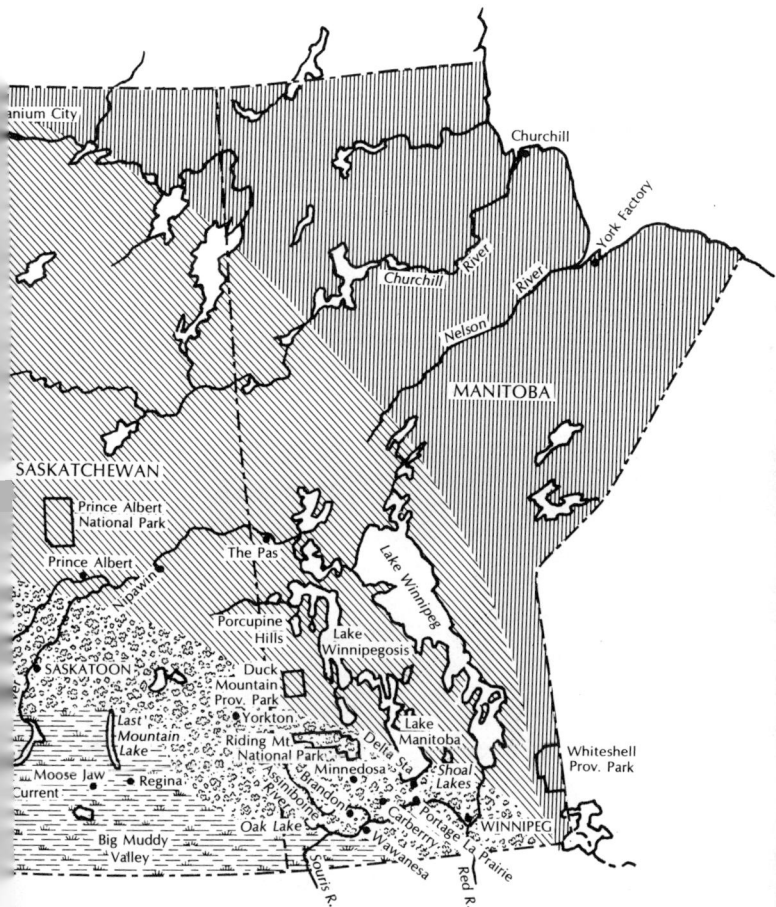

Churchill

York Factory

Churchill River

Nelson River

MANITOBA

SASKATCHEWAN

anium City

Prince Albert
National Park

Prince Albert

The Pas

Nipawin

Lake Winnipeg

Porcupine
Hills

Lake
Winnipegosis

SASKATOON

Duck
Mountain
Prov. Park

Last
Mountain
Lake

Yorkton

Lake
Manitoba

Whiteshell
Prov. Park

Riding Mt.
National Park

Delta Sta.

Moose Jaw

Minnedosa

Shoal
Lakes

Assiniboine River

Current

Regina

Brandon

Portage La Prairie

WINNIPEG

Oak Lake

Carberry

Big Muddy
Valley

Souris R.

Wawanesa

Red R.

45

marshes close to Regina City, is one of the most renowned sanctuaries in North America and it supports many millions of birds. To the farmer the area is the 'Bread-basket of the World'; to the birder the lush potholes are the 'Duck Factory of North America', and produce over fifty percent of the waterfowl. A few yards away Sage Grouse or Lark Bunting move among the dessicated stubble.

The northern barrier to man and bird is climate. The Transition or Parkland Zone, where Prairies and Boreal Forest intermix follows approximately the July 60° isotherm. In or near this esthetically more appealing diversity of habitats most of the major cities are situated. High-gliding hawks circle in time to the meadowlarks' song over the patchwork of forest and field. Northward further on the plains, the

AMERICAN WIDGEON   Richard Wright

CANADA GOOSE GOSLING   Tom W. Hall

Boreal Forest of spruce and aspen extends hundreds of miles, until the stunted trees give way to the Tundra. The forest birds; the Great Gray Owl, Sharp-shinned Hawk, Cape May Warbler, Pine Grosbeak breed around the deeper lakes which support the diving ducks; the Common Goldeneye, Bufflehead, Surf Scoter and Common Merganser.

The Canadian Shield, the third major geographical region of the provinces is also largely occupied by the Boreal Forest in the south and Tundra in the north. The proximity of the great body of water, Hudson Bay, further diversifies the bird list with a combination of true sea birds and arctic birds.

ALBERTA 🥬

Alberta provides a fascinating spectrum of areas for the birder. It covers 255,285 square miles and has great lakes, Athabasca and Lesser Slave; great rivers, Athabasca and Peace; and a great mountain chain, the Rockies. Biotically, the plains are composed of the Prairies, Parkland and Boreal Forest.

TRUMPETER SWAN   Richard Wright

The rare and striking Trumpeter Swan breeds on some of the smaller lakes west and north of Grande Prairie.

EDMONTON

The Edmonton Bird Club recommends a walk through the riverside woods. There is a trail west of the High Level Bridge which leads to White Mud Creek. A good variety of species may be seen, including several species of thrushes, warblers and vireos; Pileated Woodpeckers, and occasionally Western Tanagers and crossbills.

JUNCTION OF ATHABASCA
AND PEMBINA RIVERS

Arriving at Fawcett you enter an area of sandhill ridges, lakes and muskeg. Watch for Sandhill Cranes, Great Gray Hawk and Boreal Owls, Spruce Grouse. Three-toed and Pileated Woodpeckers, Bohemian Waxwings, as well as many warblers, thrushes and sparrows. Common Loons and Ring-necked Ducks may be found breeding in some of the lakes.

JASPER NATIONAL PARK

The 'mountain parks' provide exciting birding, provided you are willing to work. Look for Barrow's Goldeneye and other waterfowl on Talbot Lake. Also recommended is a visit to the park naturalist, who will supply you with a check list and hints on good areas. Perhaps the best spot for variety is Maligne Lake and the trails leading up to the alpine meadows. At the lake you may see Townsend's Solitaire, Clark's Nutcrackers, Steller's Jays. Hike up higher and you may find Gray-crowned Rosy Finches, Golden-crowned Sparrows, White-tailed Ptarmigan and Water Pipits.

PEYTO LAKE

Peyto Lake is on the Banff-Jasper Highway. The well marked trail allows the birder to see many sub-alpine species with relative ease. Including, for example, Varied Thrush, Gray Jay, White-tailed Ptarmigan, Gray-crowned Rosy Finch, Brewer's Sparrow, Oregon Junco, Northern Three-toed Woodpecker and several other species.

BANFF NATIONAL PARK

There are exciting walking trails which yield many new species. Once again check with the park naturalist. Among the birds found in Banff are Harlequin

GOSHAWK   Tom W. Hall

BUFFLEHEAD DUCKS   Tom W. Hall

Duck, Golden Eagle, Blue and Spruce Grouse, Pygmy Owl, Black Swift, Rufous Hummingbird, Hammond's Flycatcher, Raven, Mountain and Boreal Chickadee, Audubon's Warbler, Mac-Gillivray's Warbler, Western Tanager, Oregon Junco, Golden-crowned and Fox Sparrow.

WILDHORSE

This area of sage brush flats is located on Highway 48 south of Cypress Hills. Of special interest is the Sage Grouse. Other species of note include the Brewer's Sparrow, McCown's Longspur and Lark Bunting.

CYPRESS HILLS PARK

To reach Cypress Hills Park, go south on Highway 48 from Medicine Hat. Interesting species to be found are Black Tern, Long-billed Marsh Wren, Yellow-headed Blackbird, Red Crossbills, Mac-Gillivray's and Audubon's Warblers, Oregon Junco and White-crowned Sparrow.

SASKATCHEWAN

Dr. Stuart Houston wrote: 'Those who expect to find an arid, flat treeless plain with endless miles of waving grain are in for a surprise.' Two thirds of Saskatchewan's 251,700 square miles, is forested and offers a wide variety of habitat.

PIAPOT — CRANE LAKE

If you drive north of Piapot in summer you may see Upland Plover, Ferruginous Hawks and Black-billed Magpies. Walk to Crane Lake and you should spot Avocets, Willets, Marbled Godwits and out on the islands are colonies of California Gulls, White Pelicans and Double-crested Cormorants. On the way to and from the lake you may discover Chestnut-collared and McCown's Longspurs and Long-billed Curlews.

WHITE PELICANS   Richard Wright

CYPRESS HILLS PROVINCIAL PARK

Cypress Hills Provincial Park is located on Highway 21, about 20 miles south of Maple Creek. The Cypress Hills are the highest elevations in the province. The flora include many alpine plants. Some of the most interesting birds of the 200 species found in the park are: Red Crossbills, Audubon's, Mac-Gillivray's and Orange-crowned Warblers, Oregon Juncos, Dusky Flycatchers, and Brewer's and White-crowned Sparrows. Sage Grouse are sometimes observable on the sage plains south of the park. The park staff will supply a list of birds and advise on the best areas for birding.

SAGE GROUSE   Tom Willock

THE BADLANDS

Two areas are recommended, the Big Muddy Valley south of Regina, and the South Saskatchewan River Valley north and east of Swift Current. There you may see nesting Golden Eagles, Prairie Falcons and Rock Wrens. Also found here are Mountain Blue-birds and in some of the more restricted coulees, Yellow-breasted Chats.

GOLDEN EAGLE   Niall Rankin

DUCK MOUNTAIN PROVINCIAL PARK

The park is located 70 miles from Yorkton and includes a tongue of coniferous forest. You may see Common Loons, Red-necked Grebes and Ravens along with all the vireos, warblers and sparrows found in the Canadian Life Zone.

NIPAWIN

A very rich bird area exists along the Saskatchewan River on Highways 6, 3 and 35 north of Regina. This is the Transition or Parkland Zone with coniferous forests to the north and prairies to the south. This area is on the southern edge of the breeding range for Fox, Swamp, and Lincoln's Sparrows, Boreal Chickadee, Rusty Blackbird, Swainson's and Hermit Thrushes. Tennessee, Wilson's, Canada and Mourning Warblers, Raven, Gray Jay, Pileated Woodpecker and Spruce Grouse also occur here. Maurice Street has found nests or flightless young, of 141 species within twenty miles of Nipawin.

GREATER PRAIRIE CHICKEN   Kathleen Morck

PRINCE ALBERT NATIONAL PARK

The park is located north of Prince Albert and is a good place to see and hear many species of warbler and thrush as well as nesting Bald Eagles and Ospreys.

LAST MOUNTAIN LAKE

The north end of last Mountain Lake, 95 miles from

Regina, is Canada's first bird sanctuary. In late August and early September you may see and hear thousands of Sandhill Cranes flying from the marshes to the grain fields. You may, with much diligence, see the rare Whooping Crane during the spring of fall migration in late April or early October. This area is also good for observing waterfowl.

SANDHILL CRANE   Tom W. Hall

GREAT HORNED OWL ON RABBIT

NORTHERN SASKATCHEWAN

You may some day wish to venture further north, perhaps by air, to such places as Uranium City and Stony Rapids on Lake Athabasca.

This is boreal forest or Taiga country where spruce and Lodgepole Pine forests are interspersed with bogs and aspen thickets. In these extensive forests breed the cyclic populations of Gos Hawks that migrate southward in winter across the prairies. Spruce and Ruffed Grouse, Pine Grosbeaks, Magnolia Warblers and Slate-coloured Juncos breed across the Taiga. The lakes support Common and Red-breasted Mergansers, White-winged Scoters, Common Goldeneye and Bufflehead.

MANITOBA

Since Manitoba extended northward in 1912 to the 60th parallel, it has become a maritime province. Manitoba is 251,000 square miles in area with considerable coastline along Hudson Bay. The province is essentially flat with some hilly tracts such as the Porcupine and Riding Mountains. Over ten percent of the country is under water.

Of the total 518 bird species recorded in Canada, about 340 species are to be found in Manitoba. Of these, 274 are believed to occur each year, the others being considered irregular or accidental visitors.

SOUTHERN MANITOBA

Down in the south-western part of the province can be found beautiful sand dunes with a wide variety of bird life. These are the Carberry Hills. Oak Lake is a good spot for waterfowl as is the Souris River near Wawanesa. There are, of course, many other areas where there is good birding. Favored spots include Bird's Hill Park north of Winnipeg, Riding Mountain Park, the Red River Valley running through Winnipeg, as well as Whiteshell Provincial Park and many small pockets of woods found throughout southern Manitoba.

DELTA WATERFOWL STATION AND DELTA MARSHES

The Delta Marshes, famed throughout North America, are located at the south end of Lake Manitoba, north from Portage la Prairie. On the way you

SCAUP DUCK   David Hancock

may see Franklin's Gulls, Sprague's Pipits and Cliff
Swallows. The marshes are nesting grounds for Redhead, Canvasback, Shoveller, Green and Blue-
winged Teal, Pintail, scaup, Mallard, Ring-necked
Duck and others. White Pelicans are often spotted,
while one of the highlights of the trip are the Trumpeter Swans which breed in captivity. The Delta
Station welcomes visitors. Secure permission and
drive out along the road running east from the Delta
Station as far as it goes into the marsh for best birding. A highly recommended prerequisite is the classic
The Canvasback on a Prairie Marsh by the retired
director of the Delta Station, Dr. H. A. Hochbaum.

WESTERN GREBE   Niall Rankin

SHOAL LAKES

The Shoal Lakes, located north-east of Winnipeg, are
excellent areas for shorebirds such as Avocets, Piping
Plovers, Marbled Godwits and many other waterfowl.

MINNEDOSA POTHOLES

Surrounding the town of Minnedosa are thousand of
pothole lakes or ponds which are some of the most
productive waterfowl breeding areas of the prairies.
Driving through the area and stopping at each pothole you may with luck, see Redhead, Canvasback,
teal, scaup, Pintail, Coot and several rails. The best
time for this venture is mid April to June. You may
wish to include a spotting scope and a copy of
Kortright's *Ducks, Geese and Swans of North
America.*

CHURCHILL

Churchill is becoming widely known as one of the best places in North America to sample Arctic bird life. This area combines the tundra, taiga and tidewater. You can take the train from Winnipeg or The Pas, or fly with Transair.

With a little luck you may see some 90 different species of birds and, if you have the knack, you may discover 20 or more nesting species. The more interesting species are: Harris' Sparrow, Golden Plover, Hudsonian Godwit, Arctic Loon, Blackpoll Warbler, Lapland Longspur, Parasitic Jaeger, Whimbrel, Dunlin, Willow Ptarmigan, and Hoary and Common Redpolls.

Recommended sighting areas around Churchill are Landing Lake, Cape Merry, Twin Lakes, south of the Rocket Range, and the tundra along the road beyond the Auroral Observatory and the coastline near Bird Cove. Take rubber hip boots and lots of insect repellent.

FEMALE YELLOW-HEADED BLACKBIRD   Richard Wright

BIRDING IN ONTARIO AND QUEBEC 🦜🦜🦜

By Jim Woodford

Ontario and Quebec make up about one-third of Canada, with a total of 1,007,442 square miles. Both are dominated by the Boreal Forest which covers about four-fifths of the land mass. It is estimated that 350 million pairs of wood warblers nest in this forest. Agriculture and progress have so obliterated any trace of the natural Carolinian and Alleghanian Zones that it is more Southern Hardwood Zone. Both provinces have extensive coastlines — Ontario on the Great Lakes; Quebec on the Atlantic; and both share the shores of James and Hudson Bays.

COMMON TERNS   Eric Hosking

Eric Hosking

There are over one million square miles to cover and therefore this guide will provide just the briefest introduction to the region and a few details about the best birding areas, as well as references to further information.

ONTARIO

Ontario stretches a thousand miles from east to west and one thousand and fifty miles from north to south. Southern deciduous forest occurs in a narrow belt along Lake Erie and the west end of Lake Ontario. To the north along Hudson Bay there is a corridor of true tundra. And in between there is a mosaic of 250,000 lakes, rivers, forest — the Canadian Shield. Ontario offers great variety to the student of nature; prickly pear cactus grows in the south, polar bears roam in the north.

Winter is a good time to begin birding in Ontario. While there are fewer species present, there is usually a good variety to provide the beginner with a 'field course' in bird identification. Many species of waterfowl winter along the Great Lakes and the Niagara River; hawks and owls are found in open, farm areas; winter finches like Redpolls, Pine Siskins, crossbills, and grosbeaks are common forest species; and bird feeders attract chickadees, nuthatches, Cardinals, Blue Jays, and others.

SNOW GEESE   David Hancock

RUBY-CROWNED KINGLET TRAPPED ON BURDOCK   W. V. Crich

A highlight of the birder's year is the annual Christmas bird count held in a two-week period during the Christmas season. The combined total for southern Ontario is usually 120-140 species and about 300,000 individual birds.

Spring comes early for the Ontario birder. Horned Larks arrive back from the South in February, the harbingers of a steady stream of migrants that lasts until mid June. Fall also begins early, as migrant shorebirds may be seen by mid July. May is the best month for observing migrants, the peak in southern Ontario is about May 10. Early morning is the best time to see and hear these southern arrivals and many bird clubs sponsor a series of May walks.

For further, more detailed information the fine book *a naturalist's Guide to Ontario* edited by W. W. Judd and J. M. Speirs is highly recommended.

Now let us look at some of the best birding spots in Ontario.

ONTARIO
AND QUEBEC 🌿

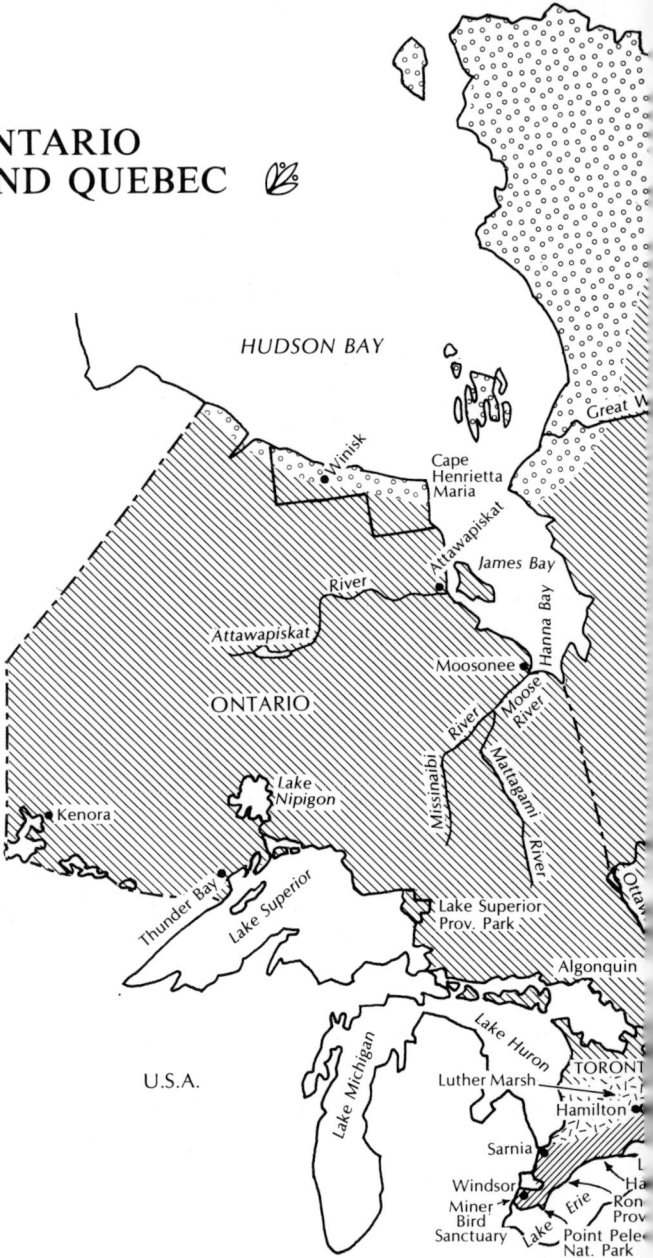

HUDSON BAY

Great W

Winisk

Cape
Henrietta
Maria

Attawapiskat

James Bay

River

Attawapiskat

Hanna Bay

Moosonee

ONTARIO

Missinaibi River

Moose River

Mattagami River

*Lake
Nipigon*

Otta

• Kenora

Thunder Bay

Lake Superior
Prov. Park

Lake Superior

Algonquin

Lake Huron

U.S.A.

TORONT

Lake Michigan

Luther Marsh

Hamilton •

Sarnia •

Ha
Ron
Prov

Windsor
Miner
Bird
Sanctuary

Lake Erie

Point Pelee
Nat. Park

River

LABRADOR

QUEBEC

St. Lawrence River

Bonaventure Is.
Perce

Laurentide
Prov. Park

Cape Tourment

Mont Tremblant
Park

QUEBEC

Gatineau
Park

iver

OTTAWA   MONTREAL

Ontario

Presqu''ile Prov. Park

ake

Niagara River

Rockhouse Point

Point Abino

Point

Cliff

k

KEY TO LIFE ZONES
FOR MAP OF
ONTARIO AND QUEBEC

Arctic

Boreal

Southern Hardwoods

Alleghanian

Carolinian

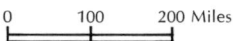

0   100   200 Miles

67

SOUTHERN ONTARIO

This region has the richest fauna of any part of Ontario, reflecting the diversity of habitats available.

PIED-BILLED GREBE   Eric Hosking

RONDEAU PROVINCIAL PARK

Rondeau is one of the best examples of southern deciduous woodland in Canada. It is a good migration area in May and September. Long ponds between raised beaches offer nesting sites for such rarities as Prothonotary Warblers, Acadian Flycatchers and Louisiana Waterthrushes. The beaches are noted for shorebird concentrations and there is an extensive marsh. These are located south of Blenheim on Highway 3.

MINER BIRD SANCTUARY

You may witness one of Ontario's most impressive gatherings of geese at the Miner ponds located about three miles west of Kingsville. April and October through December are the best months.

POINT PELEE NATIONAL PARK

If there is a birders' shrine in Canada, it is Point Pelee. There is nothing quite like a May morning on the Point. You may see over 100 species of birds; perhaps twenty-five to thirty of these being warblers. May is the best time to visit Pelee for the spring migration; May 12 is about the peak of movement. October and September are best for the spectacular fall hawk migrations. Point Pelee is south of Leamington, and is the southernmost point of the mainland of Canada. The National Parks Service operates an excellent bird lists and information.

CANADA GOOSE   Tom W. Hall

HAWK CLIFF

To reach Hawk Cliff take a southerly route from St. Thomas on Highway 4 to Union, then turn east for one and one-quarter miles and then turn right to the lakeshore. At Hawk Cliff it is possible to see more hawks in one day than any other place in North America. Broadwings are the most common, a peak number of 70,000 was seen on September 16, 1961. About 16 species may be seen at the Cliff and peak flights generally occur between September 10 to September 23.

LUTHER MARSH

One of the best spots to see marsh birds and water-fowl; Luther Marsh is located about thirty miles from Kitchener. This is an extensive marsh where Red-head, Ruddy, Gadwell and many other more common duck species breed. This marsh also houses one of the largest heronries in the province, with nesting Green, Great Blue, and Night Herons, as well as American and Cattle Egrets. A canoe is essential to see much of this area.

BALD EAGLE   David Hancock

ROUGH-LEGGED HAWK   David Hancock

LONG POINT

The Bay is famous as a stop-over for migration water-fowl, especially period is from mid-March to late April. Other species, such as Canvasbacks and Red-heads are also common. Long Point is a twenty mile sand-spit sticking out into the middle of Lake Erie. It is accessible only by boat on a four-wheel drive vehicle. Canada's largest bird banding and passerine bird research station is located at the tip of the Point.

For information write: Long Point Bird Observatory, 116 Three Valleys Drive, Don Mills.

ROCKHOUSE POINT AND POINT ABINO

The shoreline of Lake Erie from Fort Erie west is one of the finest areas to observe migrant shorebirds from mid July to October. The best plan is to follow the road along the shore and stop at every opportunity to scan the shoreline.

AMERICAN BITTERN   W. V. Crich

NIAGARA RIVER

This famed river is a great spot to observe diving
ducks, grebes and gulls, and of course, terns. Look
for Forter's, Caspian and Black Terns; Bonaparte's,
Little and Franklin's Gulls; and occasional rarities
such as the Kittiwake. A winter drive along the River
from Niagara-on-the-Lake to Fort Erie often pro-
duces some surprises.

PRESQU'ILE PROVINCIAL PARK

Located south of Brighton, Presqu'ile offers a good
variety of habitats; a fine marsh, beaches, and mudflats as well as offshore islands used as nesting
grounds by gulls and terns.

LAKE SUPERIOR PROVINCIAL PARK

Found north of Sault Ste. Marie, the park offers
beautiful shoreline scenery. Many of the species listed
for Algonquin may be found in this park.

NORTHERN ONTARIO

The major difficulty to birding in northern Ontario is access. There are dozens of good areas, but getting to them may difficult and expensive. There is now a series of provincial parks along Highway 11 and these afford travellers opportunities to sample northern Ontario birds. Canoe trips along northern rivers may be exciting and provide sightings of breeding birds such as Golden Eagles and Peregrine Falcons, which are seldom seen in the southern part of the province. Farther north Winisk Park and the Attawapiskat and Moose river areas are recommended. Information on these and others is available from

OSPREY   Eric Hosking

ALGONQUIN PROVINCIAL PARK

Algonquin is Ontario's second largest park, 2,700 square miles. Its high altitude gives it a colder climate and more northern fauna and flora. In summer the earnest birder may turn up Ravens, Gray Jays, Olive-sided Flycatchers, Boreal Chickadees, Spruce Grouse, Blackbacked Three-toed Woodpeckers, Evening Grosbeaks, and many more. A winter visit is often rewarding with large flocks of winter finches along the highway and trails (take snowshoes!). The Ontario Ministry of Natural Resources has a fine park museum and staff naturalists will supply check-lists and information.

SPRUCE GROUSE   David Hancock

the Ministry of Natural Resources, Parliament Buildings, Toronto, Ontario.

SNOWY OWL   Eric Hosking

MOOSONEE

This tidewater community is reached by the Polar Bear Express train from Cochrane. White-crowned and Fox Sparrows nest here. Palm and Orange-crowned Warblers sometimes are found, though sparingly. In spring and fall, spectacular numbers of waterfowl and shorebirds gather on the famous lowlands near the mouth of the Moose River and up the coast. Shipsands Island is one of the best observation points. Hannah Bay is a staging area for Blue Geese. It is possible to arrange travel by aircraft or canoe at Moosonee. Contact the local Ministry of Natural Resources office.

CAPE HENRIETTA MARIA —
POLAR BEAR PROVINCIAL PARK

This is Ontario's largest park and is found at the junction of James and Hudson Bays. There is a breeding colony of Blue and Snow Geese near Kwinabiskak Lake. Polar Bear Park is accessible only by boat or aircraft. It affords the Ontario birder an opportunity to sample the Arctic in their own province. King Eiders, Dunlins, Pectoral, Stilt, and Semipalmated Sandpipers, Golden Plovers, Northern Phalaropes, Parasitic Jaegers and Lapland Longspurs have all been found nesting in the Park. Gyr Falcons and Snowy Owls are common visitors that may eventually be found nesting in the Park.

PECTORAL SANDPIPER   Niall Rankin

SEMI-PALMATED PLOVER   Richard Wright

QUEBEC

Quebec is the largest of Canada's provinces, stretching 1,200 miles from the international boundary to Cape Childlay on Hudson Strait. Nearly 71,000 square miles are covered by lakes and rivers and 160,000 square miles are covered with dwarf forest and tundra. Quebec has more than 5,000 miles of coastline and the magnificent St. Lawrence River traverses much of the southern region.

Bird study here has never enjoyed the popularity it does elsewhere in Canada, but some of the most spectacular North American sights of birding, such as the Gannets of Bonaventure Island and the Snow Geese of Cap Tourments are to be seen in this area.

BLUE AND SNOW GEESE   Edgar Jones

CAP TOURMENTS

This stopover point for Snow Geese is located some thirty miles east of Quebec City. Earl Godfrey in *Birds of Canada* suggests that the whole population of the sub-species *atlantica* stops over here, possibly 50,000 individuals. In fall, the first Snows arrive about mid September and their numbers continue to increase until mid October. Spring arrival is late March and the birds remain until early May.

YELLOW-THROAT WARBLERS   W. Goodpaster

BLACK-CAPPED CHICKADEE   W. V. Crich

MONT TREMBLANT PARK

Mont Tremblant is a large park with a variety of habitats and is located about seventy-five miles north of Montreal. It offers the birder an opportunity to observe many species of warbler, loon, thrush, and sparrow on their breeding grounds. There are also birds like the Boreal Chickadee, Raven, Three-toed Woodpecker and Spruce and Ruffed Grouse feeding here.

BARN SWALLOWS   David Hancock

BELTED KINGFISHERS   W. V. Crich

LAURENTIDE PROVINCIAL PARK

This park is situated in the Boreal Forest region of
Canada and is an excellent place to see and hear nesting warblers. It has been estimated that there is one
pair of nesting warblers per acre of forest! Species
include Black-throated Green, Bay-breasted, Cape
May, Tennessee, Magnolia and Blackburnian
Warblers. Kinglets and thrushes are also to be spied
here.

ST. LAWRENCE RIVER

There are good birding spots all along the St.
Lawrence where one may see waterfowl, shorebirds,

various species of gull, and terns. Closer to the mouth, seabirds may sometimes be seen. A trip along the north shore takes the birder through some varied country, climaxed by some tundralike areas near Sept-Iles which houses many characteristically northern birds. We recommend late June and July.

BONAVENTURE AND PERCE

Bonaventure Island is famous throughout North America for its nesting Gannets and other seabirds. It is reached by boat from the village of Perce. It is estimated that between 7,000 and 10,000 Gannets nest in this area. To reach the nesting cliffs you must walk across the island. Some of the Gannets nest on top of cliffs, which if climbed afford excellent views and numerous opportunities for photography. Other species you may chance to see include Common Puffins, kittiwakes, Razor-billed Auks, Common Murres, Black Guillemots and Herring Gulls. Many other species occur on the island and in the island woods.

COMMON PUFFINS   Barry Ranford

81

BIRDING IN THE ATLANTIC PROVINCES 🐦🐦🐦

The character of oceans is deeply impressed upon the Atlantic Provinces. Over 10,000 miles of shoreline separate the plankton rich water from the often harsh and poor soiled land. The land can be divided into three major life zones. The richest soils support the hardwood forests of the Alleghanian Zone of the Fundy Trough, which in turn today supports mixed farming and the most diversified bird life. The largest area of these eastern provinces is covered by Boreal Forest. In northern Newfoundland trees give way to

COMMON MURRE   David Hancock

true Arctic Tundra. Through poor forestry and agricultural practices, much of the forest cover has been reduced to treeless heather bogs, a story similar to the destruction of Scotland's forests and their replacement by heather moors.

The natural physical borders greatly influence people and birds. On the east the mainland mass of the Applachian Mountains form a barrier, and to the north, the Gulf of St. Lawrence and the barren headlands of Quebec are uninviting to man or bird. Singularly the greatest feature influencing life in the Atlantic Provinces is not land features but the Grand Banks, 50,000 square miles of shallow waters where fish team. From the north the plankton rich Labrador Current brings down cold water. From the south the Gulf Stream brings up warm water. These mix over the Grand Banks to form a rich broth of plankton, fish, seals, seabirds and fishermen.

Seabirds, Common Puffins, Murres, petrels and Gannets, abandon the expanses of the open sea to congregate on offshore islands and isolated headlands to raise their young. From Grand Manan to Funk Island the sight, sound and smell of these rookeries is unexcelled in the bird world.

Arctic migrants also greatly enrich the bird fauna. The Golden Plover make the great shallows of the Bay of Fundy their last feeding place before the non-stop flight to Patagonia. The white sands of Prince Edward Island and the meadows of crowberries of each province attract millions of arctic nesting shorebirds. The arctic Peregrine Falcon stop over here to feed on these migrants. Over 325 bird species inhabit the Atlantic provinces.

ATLANTIC PROVINCES

Stephen

S

ANTICOSTI ISLAND

GULF OF

ST. LAWRENCE

Bonaventure Is.

Perce

Magalen Islands

High
Nat.

Chaleur Bay

QUEBEC

P.E.I. Prov. Park

P.E.I.

Charlottet

Northumberland Str.

Southwest Miramichi River

Midgic
Marsh

Tantramar
Marsh

NEW BRUNSWICK

SCOTIA

Fredricton

Odell Park

Red Head
Marsh

Point Lepreau

St. John

Chamecook

St. Andrews

St. John
Harbour

Grand Pre

Evangiline
Beach

Bay of Fundy

NOVA

H

U.S.A.

Maces Bay

Grand
Manan

Lake George

Yarmouth

Cape Sable

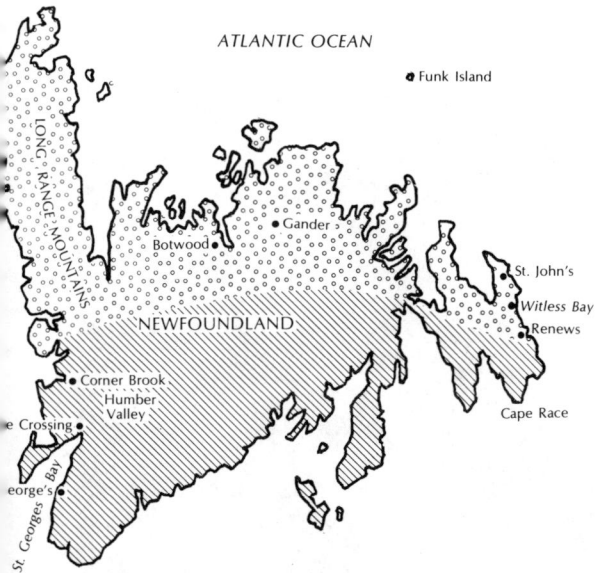

ATLANTIC OCEAN

⚬ Funk Island

LONG RANGE MOUNTAINS

Botwood ●
● Gander

St. John's ●
Witless Bay
Renews

NEWFOUNDLAND

● Corner Brook
Humber Valley

Cape Race

e Crossing ●

eorge's ●

St. George's Bay

Bras D'Or

CAPE BRETON
ISLAND

ATLANTIC OCEAN

AX

KEY TO LIFE ZONES
FOR MAP OF
THE ATLANTIC PROVINCES

Arctic

Boreal

Alleghanian

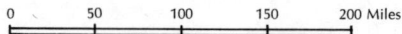

0   50   100   150   200 Miles

GREEN HERON   W. Goodpaster

NEW BRUNSWICK

Like the economy of the province, the bird fauna of
New Brunswick draws its greatest interest and wealth
from the surrounding seas. The plankton rich seas
feed millions of small fish which in turn feed the
millions of sea birds. The most famous seabird areas
are the shores of Gaspe, Bonaventure I., and the Bay
of Fundy islands, Grand Manan and the smaller
surrounding archipelago.

RED HEAD MARSH

The east side of St. John Harbour, two miles along the shore road beyond the dry dock, is an excellent spot for shorebirds, waders and ducks, from early spring to late into the fall. Unusual species to be seen include Common Egret, Pintail, American Widgeon, and Common Gallinule.

TANTRAMAR MARCH

Between Sackville and Amherst is a large diked marsh. It is mostly open meadows where Short-eared Owls and Marsh Hawks are residents. In the fall Rough-legged Hawks and Snowy Owls can be common. Rails — Clapper, Sora and Virginia — may be found in Tantramar and other marshes along the coast.

COOT FEEDING YOUNG   Tom W. Hall

MIDGIC MARSH

Several unusual species of marsh birds may be found in this marsh located at the head of the Tantramar River. The Yellow Rail has been found, along with breeding Short-billed and Long-billed Marsh Wrens.

COMMON GUILLEMOT   Eric Hosking

RAZORBILL   Barry Ranford

COMMON PUFFIN   Barry Ranford

GRAND MANAN AND MACHIAS SEAL ISLAND

The Arctic current maintains a cool summer climate and numerous species are to be found here that are not seen again until you are several hundred miles north. On Grand Manan you may see Leach's Petrel, Black Guillemots, Arctic Terns and eiders. These may also be seen on most of the smaller islands in the area. Perhaps the best of these is Machais Seal Island, now a migratory bird sanctuary. There you may see 1,000 Atlantic Puffins, 200 Razor-billed Auks, 3,000 Common and Arctic Terns and Leach's Petrels. In late summer and early fall you may find accidental waifs, such as Prairie and Connecticut Warblers, Lark Buntings and Yellow-breasted Chats, along the shore.

ST. ANDREWS, CHAMOOK, POINT LEPREAU

Wintering water birds, including Arctic species, gather in large numbers from early fall to late spring; birds such as eiders, alcids (Razorbills and Common

89

Murres), Great Cormorants, Common and Red-throated Loons. At Mace's Bay, a number of Brant gather in April and early May.

ST. JOHN HARBOUR

Some of the breeding waterfowl of New Brunswick such as Black Duck, Common Goldeneye, Common and Red-breasted Mergansers; along with large flocks of Herring, Black-backed, Glaucous and Iceland Gulls, winter in the harbour.

NORTHUMBERLAND STRAIT, GULF OF ST. LAWRENCE, BAIE DE CHALEUR

All along the seacoast there are sandy bars, beaches and mudflats where great numbers of shorebirds congregate in search of food. Spring migration lasts into June and the first fall migrants return at the end of July. August is recommended by W. Austin Squires of the New Brunswick Museum, as the best time to see Yellowlegs, Dowitchers, Turnstones, Knots and plovers; Black-bellied, Piping, Semi-palmated and of course 'peeps', the small sandpiper which always presents a challenge to the beginner.

COMMON MURRE   David Hancock

BALD EAGLE   David Hancock

ODELL PARK, FREDERICTON

The Fredericton Bird Club recommends the Park as an excellent spot for birding at all seasons. In winter there are Redpolls, Siskins, Pine Grosbeaks, nuthatches and chickadees, and in spring the warbler migration is spectacular.

NEWFOUNDLAND

Islands are traditionally exceptional places to find birds and Newfoundland is no exception. Harold Horwood wrote in *Canadian Audubon:* 'Anyone looking for strays from Europe and the Gulf of Mexico would be hard put to find a better place for his activities than Newfoundland's southern shore, a 70 mile strip of coast running from St. John's to Cape Race. Newfoundland contains about 42,000 square miles; its greatest north-south length is 350 miles, and its average breadth is 130 miles. Its surface is diversified by barrens, mountains, marshes, ponds and lakes. Its seas are rich in fish and bird life.

ST. JOHN'S TO CAPE RACE

Every spring during mid April, small birds move north *en masse* and occasionally 'overshoot' Cape Cod to end up along the south shore of Newfoundland. Birds such as Scarlet Tanagers, Indigo Buntings, Glossy Ibises, European Golden Plovers, and the first Cattle Egret for North America — and on it goes.

WITLESS BAY

It is about twenty miles from St. John to this wonderful gathering place. In summer, seabirds such as Razor-billed Auks, Dovekies, Black Guillemots, Puffins and Leach's Petrels nest here by the score. Kittiwakes, Arctic and Common Terns and murres also nest in this area.

LONG RANGE MOUNTAINS

The mountains in western Newfoundland rise to a height of 2,000 feet, with an Arctic-Alpine microclimate in some places. The birder may experience a variety of habitats if he is willing to climb a little. Bird life changes from birds such as grackles, swallows, and robins, through Boreal Forest species such as finches and warblers, to tundra-like birds such as the Horned Larks, pipits, and large hawks, like the Gyr falcon.

RENEWS OR CHANCE COVE

Chance Cove is a good place to observe migrant shorebirds in August and September. As many as twenty species may be seen in one day, including

Whimbrels, Golden Plovers, Knots, Black-bellied Plovers and Northern and Red Phalaropes.

STEPHENVILLE CROSSING TO ST. GEORGE'S

There are vast tidal flats around the end of St. George's Bay between Stephenville Crossing and St. George's. During the fall migration hundreds of thousands of shorebirds may be observed resting and feeding.

COMMON GRACKLES   Eric Hosking

HUMBER VALLEY

Located north and east of Corner Brook, this valley is a good place to observe nesting waterfowl such as Canada Geese, Common Goldeneye; Black Duck,

Common and Red-breasted Mergansers, the Black-backed Three-toed Woodpecker and the Boreal Owl.

Over 200 species of birds have been sighted in Newfoundland, of these about 140 species are considered as common residents, or regular visitors, and may be seen regularly in the appropriate habitat.

FUNK ISLAND

Funk Island, 40 miles at sea, is one of the most spectacular sights that a birder will ever experience. It was the last breeding ground of the now extinct Great Auk. There are large breeding populations of Atlantic Murres, Razor-billed Auks, Thick-billed Murres, Gannets and puffins. This island is reached only by boat and visitors must be prepared for a stay of several days, if the weather turns foul. In 1936, 14 Gannets established here. Today several thousand pairs nest here, possibly reflecting a warmer climate and the northward movement of mackerel.

LONG-TAILED JAEGER   Eric Hosking

NOVA SCOTIA

OSPREY   Eric Hosking

Nova Scotia is Canada's most southeasterly province and is a long, narrow peninsula. It has an area of 21,068 square miles, is about 370 miles long, and varies in width from 50 to 100 miles. The province is largely included in the Acadian Forest Region. There is a wide variety of habitat; shorelines, ponds, rivers, abandoned farms, meadows, lakes, sand beaches and estuaries. Although Nova Scotia is Canada's second smallest province, approximately 350 species have been recorded which reflects the diversity of habitats. Of interest is that apparently, the first bird list for Nova Scotia was completed on May 20, 1604, by Samuel de Champlain. Sable Island, 100 miles off the coast, is known to sailors for the 500 ships and 5,000 lives it has taken. It is known to birders as the only breeding area for the very rare Ipswich Sparrow.

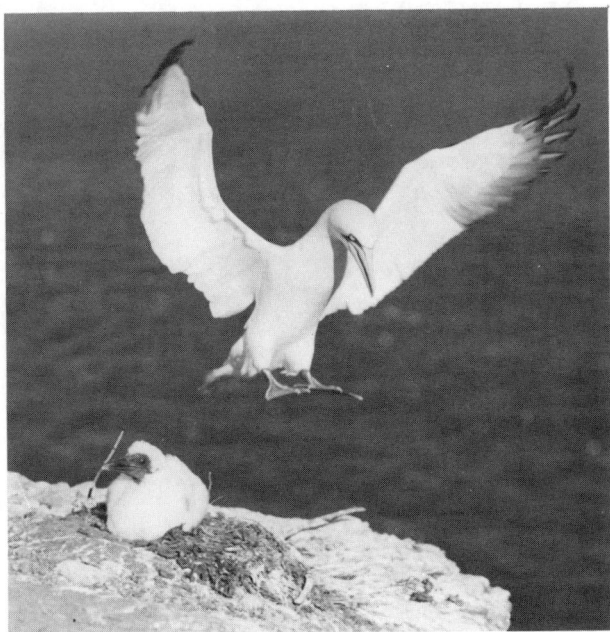

GANNET

SEA BIRD COLONIES

There are many colonies of breeding sea birds in Nova Scotia. Species such as Leach's Petrels, Great and Double-crested Cormorants, Common and Arctic Terns, Great Black-backed Gulls and Great Blue Herons. The Museum in Halifax will recommend the best colony closest to your area.

BIRD ISLANDS

The islands may be reached by boat from Big Bras d'Or. Situated on the islands are breeding colonies of

Puffins and Razorbill Auks. The best time to observe the birds rearing young is, of course, late May, June and July.

EVANGELINE BEACH

Evangeline Beach is located at North Grand Pre, and is one of the best beaches to see concentrations of migrating shorebirds during early August.

LAKE GEORGE

The lake is located about ten miles from Yarmouth. The largest breeding colony of Great Black-backed Gulls in North America is located here. Also to be found hereabouts are smaller numbers of Herring Gulls, which breed in a dense, noisy crowd.

SOLITARY SANDPIPER   Jean-Louis Frund

HIGHLAND NATIONAL PARK

This strikingly beautiful park on Cape Breton affords the birder fine opportunities to see such species as Pine Grosbeaks, Greater Yellow-legs, Common Goldeneye, Bonaparte's Gull, Lincoln's Sparrows, Gray-cheeked Thrush, Cape May Warbler, Bay-breasted Warbler, Blackburnian Warbler and Mourning Warbler. You may also see some seabirds along the shores in the park if you drive around the Cabot Trail.

PEREGRINE FALCON AT EYRIE   David Hancock

DIAMOND ISLAND

Diamond Island is one of the Five Islands group located in Colchester Country. On the seaward cliff side there is a long-established eyrie of the endangered Peregrine Falcons. The eyrie may be observed from the beach below. In the fall, Peregrines from the Arctic may be seen 'buzzing' flocks of migrant shorebirds.

TUSKET ISLANDS

The Common and Arctic Terns breed on Tusket Islands, and some years there may also be observed some Roseate Terns. To reach these islands, take a boat from Lower Wedgeport.

PRINCE EDWARD ISLAND 🪶

The richer soils, surrounding seas and its location on the eastern flyway give P.E.I. an extremely rich bird fauna. In contrast to the harsh rocky terrain of adjacent Cape Breton Island, the twenty-five miles of white sandy beaches of P.E.I. National Park are good areas for gulls, tern, and shorebirds. The mixed farming areas are excellent for warblers, flycatchers and sparrows.

BIRD CLUBS

BRITISH COLUMBIA

Alouette Field Naturalists
Mrs. Duane Vandenberg
12554 Grace St.
Maple Ridge, B.C. V2X 5N2

Alpine Club of Canada
(Vancouver Island Section)
R.R. Neave
RR 2
Nanaimo, B.C.

Alpine Club of Canada
(Vancouver Section)
P.O. Box 2377
Vancouver, B.C.

Arrowsmith
Natural History Society
Mrs. Thelma Farrell
Box 421
Parksville, B.C. V0R 2S0
(604) 248-6789

British Columbia
Mountaineering Club
P.O. Box 2674
Vancouver, B.C.

Burnaby Outdoors
Education Association
Joe Sadowski
8004 Hunter St.
Burnaby, 2, B.C.

Central Okanagan Naturalist Club
Mrs. Lily Palmer
925 Bernard Ave.
Kelowna, B.C.
(604) 762-8294

Chilliwack Field Naturalists Club
John Sargeant
45466 Crescent Dr.
Chilliwack, B.C.
(604) 795-5230

Columbia Valley Naturalists
Box 9, (Mrs. Chris Schiesser)
Golden, B.C.
(604) 344-6131

Comox District
Mountaineering Club
Ruth J. Masters
RR 1
Courtenay, B.C.

Comox-Strathcona
Natural History Society
Miss Phil Capes
RR 1
Comox, B.C.
(604) 339-2708

Cowichan Valley
Natural History Society
Clarence White
5798 Alderlea St.
Duncan, B.C. V9L 3V5

Dogwood Canoe Club
7088 Nelson
Burnaby, B.C.
(604) 435-4206

Federation of
British Columbia Naturalists
Box 34246, Station D
Vancouver 9, B.C.

Federation of Mountain
Clubs of British Columbia
P.O. Box 33768
Vancouver 9, B.C.

Fort Nelson Trail & Nature Club
Fiona Donovan
Box 694
Fort Nelson, B.C. V0C 1R0

Ft. St. John Naturalists
H.J. Westheuser
9612 - 105th Ave.
Fort St. John, B.C. V1J 2M1

Island Mountain Ramblers
P.O. Box 691
Nanaimo, B.C.
(604) 753-5924

Kamloops Naturalists Club
Mr. J. Hunka
2464 Young

Kamloops, B.C.
(604) 376-9253

Kitimat Naturalists Club
Mrs. Phyllis LeBlanc
71 Wedeene St.
Kitimat, B.C. V8C 1W3

Lake Windermere Naturalists Club
A. Kraayvanger
Box 511
Windermere, B.C. V0A 1K0

Langley Field Naturalists
Mrs. Adeline Nicol
20570 - 102 Ave., RR 4
Langley, B.C. V3R 4P7

Mitlenatch Field Naturalist Society
Mrs. R. Shipway
General Delivery
Campbell River, B.C.
(604) 923-5122

Nanaimo District Naturalists
Mrs. D. Kerridge
3397 Stephenson Point Rd.
Nanaimo, B.C.
(604) 758-9727

North Okanagan Naturalists Club
Box 473
Vernon, B.C.
(604) 542-2977

Oliver-Osoyoos Naturalists Club
Mrs. Marie Pushak
RR 1
Osoyoos, B.C. V0H 1V0
(604) 495-7764

Okanagan Similkameen
Parks Society
Box 787
Summerland, B.C.
(604) 769-4249

Prince George Naturalists Club
Mrs. J. Staniland
5420 Dalhousie Dr.
Prince George, B.C. V2N 1Z9
(604) 964-7132;   563-4063

Q.C.I. Museum Society
Box 130
Masset, B.C.

Royal City Naturalists Society
Pegeen McAskill
107 Sinclair St.
New Westminster, B.C.
521-5574

Saltspring Trail and Nature Club
Mrs. J.W. McAndless
RR 1
Malaview Dr.
Ganges, B.C. V0S 1E0

Shuswap Naturalist Club
Guy A. Graham
RR 4
Salmon Arm, B.C. V0E 2T0
(604) 832-2284

Sierra Club of B.C.
(Victoria Branch)
Box 202
Victoria, B.C.

Sierra Club
(Western Canada Chapter)
3504 W. 19 Ave.
Vancouver 8, B.C.
(604) 733-6161

South Oakanagan Naturalists Club
Mrs. W.F. Gougeon
1412 Sparton Dr., RR 1
Penticton, B.C. V2A 6J6

Sunshine Coast Naturalists
Mrs. D. Hewitt
4538 Michigan Ave.
Powell River, B.C. V8A 2S7

Terrace Hiking & Naturalist Club
Mrs. Judy Gaunt
4902 Scott Ave.
Terrace, B.C. V8G 2B8

Thetis Park
Nature Sanctuary Association
W. Ron Seaborn
3552 Henderson Road
Victoria, B.C. V8P 5B1

Timberline Trail & Nature Club
Ellen Schoen
9049 Elwood Drive
Dawson Creek, B.C. V1G 3M8

Vancouver Natural History Society
Box 3021,
Vancouver 3, B.C. V6B 3X5
(604) 922-7992;   685-5131;
731-6027

Victoria Natural History Society
Box 1747
Victoria, B.C. V8W 2Y1
(604) 477-1152

**West Kootenay
 Naturalist Association**
Jim Horswill
116 - 4th Avenue S.
Box 3121
Castlegar, B.C.

White Rock Naturalists
Miss M.A. Schouten
14916 Thrift Ave.
White Rock, B.C.
(604) 536-6018

Williams Lake Field Naturalists
Box 1268,
Williams Lake, B.C.
(604) 392-5000

ALBERTA

Alberta Natural History Society
Maxine O'Riordan
41 Springfield Avenue
Red Deer, Alberta
(403) 347-4827

**Alpine Club of Canada
(Calgary Section)**
Box 1995
Calgary, Alberta

**Alpine Club of Canada
(Edmonton Section)**
A.S. Rankin,
10340 - 83rd St.
Edmonton, Alberta T6A 3P1
(403) 465-4284

Bow Valley Naturalists
Box 1693
Banff, Alberta T0L 0C0
(403) 762-4160

Buffalo Lake Naturalists
Box 881
Stettler, Alberta T0C 2L0
(403) 742-3846;   742-3840

Calgary Field Naturalists' Society
P.O. Box 981
Calgary, Alberta
(403) 249-6977

Edmonton Bird Club
Box 4441
Edmonton, Alberta T6E 4T5

Edmonton Junior Naturalists
Joy Finlay, Site 9, RR 2
Sherwood Park, Alberta T8A 3K2
(403) 467-7649

Edmonton Natural History Club
Box 1582
Edmonton, Alberta T5J 2H9
(403) 432-1420

Federation of Alberta Naturalists
Box 1472
Edmonton, Alberta T5J 2N5
(403) 435-7006

Rocky Mountain House Bird Club
Box 764
Rocky Mountain House, Alberta
(403) 845-3531

Sierra Club of Alberta
Dr. P.J. Vermeulen
3635 Utah Dr. NW
Calgary 44, Alberta
(403) 284-3490

**Skyline Trail Hikers of the
Canadian Rockies**
Box 5905, Station A
Calgary, Alberta T2H 1Y4
(403) 252-2804

**Trail Riders of
the Canadian Rockies**
Box 6742, Station D
Calgary 2, Alberta
(403) 252-2840

SASKATCHEWAN

**Indian Head Natural
History Society**

Mrs. Mary Skinner
Indian Head,
Saskatchewan S0G 2K0
(306) 695-3488; 695-3668

**Maple Creek Natural
History Society**
Miss Kate Shuard,
Box 217
Maple Creek, Saskatchewan
(306) 667-3011

Moose Jaw Natural History Society
Miss Ruth Hilling
25 - 72 Ross St. E.
Moose Jaw, Saskatchewan
(306) 693-1626

Regina Natural History Society
Box 1321
Regina, Saskatchewan S4P 3B8
(306) 523-7323; 586-5177

**Saskatchewan Natural
History Society**
Box 1121
Regina, Saskatchewan S4P 3B4

Saskatoon Natural History Society
Dr. Lynn Oliphant
330 Saskatchewan Crescent West
Saskatoon, Saskatchewan
(306) 242-4530

**Swift Current Museum
& Natural History Society**
Mrs. Clarence Wilson
Box 1477,
Swift Current, Saskatchewan
(306) 773-9888

MANITOBA

Brandon Junior Birders
Dr. John Lane
1701 Lorne Avenue
Brandon, Manitoba
(204) 727-8847

Brandon Natural History Society
Miss M. McCowan
1415 - 8th St.
Brandon, Manitoba R7A 3Z6

Manitoba Naturalists Society
Room 214

190 Rupert Ave.
Winnipeg, Manitoba R3B 0N2
(204) 943-9029

ONTARIO

**Brereton Field
Naturalists Club of Barrie**
Mrs. E. Smith
RR2
Utopia, Ontario
(705) 728-9406

Bruce Trail Association
33 Hardale Crescent
Hamilton 56, Ontario

Conservation Council of Ontario
604 - The Board of Trade Building
11 Adelaide Street West
Toronto 105, Ontario
(416) 366-1387

Federation of Ontario Naturalists
1262 Don Mills Rd.
Don Mills, Ontario
(416) 444-8419

**Georgetown and District
Naturalists Club**
10 Albert St.
Georgetown, Ontario
(416) 877-1829

**Guelph Naturalists' Club
P.O. Box 1401
Guelph, Ontario N1H 6N8**

Hamilton Naturalists' Club
P.O. Box 384
Hamilton, Ontario L8N 3C8
(416) 689-1365

Huntsville Nature Club
Box 883
Huntsville, Ontario

Ingersoll, Nature Club
Ingersoll, Ontario

Kent Nature Club
59 William St. N.
Chatham, Ontario
(519) 352-8540

Kingston Field Naturalists
P.O. Box 831
Kingston, Ontario

Kirkland Lake Nature Club
Mrs. George Honer
15 Lake Shore Rd.
Kirkland Lake, Ontario
(705) 567-3480

Kitchener-Waterloo
Field Naturalists
W.F. Cooper
317 Highland Rd. E.
Kitchener, Ontario
(519) 743-3827

Long Point Bird Observatory
116 Three Valleys Drive
Don Mills, Ontario
(416) 444-3979

Niagara Falls Nature Club
P.O. Box 522
Niagara Falls, Ontario
(416) 356-1089

Ontario Bird Banding Association
Miss Jayne E. Evans
P.O. Box 551
Midland, Ontario
(705) 549-2106

Oshawa Naturalists' Club
Box 354,
Oshawa, Ontario
(416) 987-4487

Ottawa Field-Naturalists' Club
Box 3264
Postal Station C
Ottawa, Ontario K1Y 4J5

St. Thomas Field Naturalist Club
Mrs. Eileene Stewart
6 Yarwood Street
St. Thomas, Ontario
(519) 631-0775

Sault Naturalists
Linda Evans
124 Andrew Street
Sault Ste. Marie,
Ontario P6A 1M9
(705) 254-1278

Sierra Club of Ontario
18 - 43 Victoria Street
Toronto, Ontario
(416) 366-3494

Stratford Field Naturalists Club
Mrs. Maureen P. Davis
RR 2
Stratford, Ontario N5A 6S3
(519) 273-0158

Thunder Bay Naturalists
Mrs. Ellen R. Bocking
15 Knight Street
Thunder Bay N, Ontario P7A 3M5
(807) 345 - 9869

Toronto Field Naturalists
1164 Broadview Ave.
Toronto, Ontario
(416) 422-4830

West Elgin Nature Club
Allan S. Craig
Box 129
West Lorne, Ontario N0L 2P0
(519) 768-1030

Woodstock Naturalists Society
Albert H. Cole
278 Ingersoll Ave.
Woodstock, Ontario M4S 7W8
(519) 537-6551

QUEBEC

Les Cercles Des Jeunes Naturalistes
Jardin Botanique de Montreal
4101 est, rue Sherbrooke
Montreal 406, Quebec
(514) 872-2696;   849-8141

Club Des Ornithologues
De Quebec, Inc
8191, avenue de Zoo
Orsainville, Quebec G1G 4G4
(418) 643-2310

Province of Quebec Society
for the Protection of Birds, Inc.
John Delafield
3496 Westmore Ave.
Montreal 262, Quebec
(514) 636-9865

NEW BRUNSWICK

Fredericton Field-Naturalists
c/o Prof. T. Deilworth
Department of Biology
University of N.B.
Fredericton, N.B.

Fundy Hiking Trail
521 Blythwood Ave.
Moncton, New Brunswick
(506) 386-3675

Moncton Naturalists' Club
Dr. M. Majka
Regional Lab
Arden St.
Moncton, New Brunswick

**New Brunswick Federation
of Naturalists**
277 Douglas Ave.
St. John, New Brunswick
(506) 693-1196

Purple Martin and Bird Society
P.O. Box 463
Moncton, New Brunswick
(506) 382-7692; 855-2246

Saint John Naturalists Club
c/o D.S. Christie
277 Douglas Avenue
Saint John, New Brunswick

NOVA SCOTIA

Nova Scotia Bird Society
Nova Scotia Museum
1747 Summer St.
Halifax, Nova Scotia

PRINCE EDWARD ISLAND

**Natural History Society
of Prince Edward Island**
Margaret Mallett
53 Fitzroy St.
Charlottetown,
Prince Edward Island
(902) 894-9595

NEWFOUNDLAND

**Newfoundland Natural
History Society**
P.O. Box 1013
St. John's, Newfoundland

YUKON and NORTHWEST TERRITORIES

Yukon Conservation Society
Box 4163
Whitehorse, Yukon
(403) 667-7885; 667-7131

AUDUBON
CHRISTMAS COUNTS🦢🦢

BRITISH COLUMBIA

Location	Species	Birds	Coun-ters	Comment
Campbell River: Mitlenatch Fld Nats	66	4,076	16	Rainy/sunny. Ten trumpeter Swans seen. One Anna's Hummingbird, 7 red crossbills.
Courtenay: Comox-Strathcona N.H.S.	90	15,460	—	Weather good. Peregrine Falcon, Ring-billed Gull, 67 Tr. Swan, Mourning Dove, Harris' Sparrow, Great H. Owl. Only 1 Calif. Quail.
Nanaimo: Nan. Dist. Naturalists Club	80	8,963	—	Rainy/cloudy. 23 Tr. Swans, 5 Sht-eared Owls, 8 Steller's Jays, 6 Pileated Woodpeckers, 648 Pine Siskins
Duncan: Cowichan Bird Society	105	8,743	16	Heavy rain, Mockingbird, Anna's Hummingbird, Audubon's Warbler, 2 Myrtle Warbler, Outside period — Common Scoter, Oldsquaw.
Victoria: Victoria N.H. Society	123	45,673	56	Weather variable. Ylw-billed Loon, Rusty Blackbird, White-thr. Sparrow, 4 Harris' Sparrow. Only 4 skylarks and 1 Steller's Jay.
Pender Islands: Mr. & Mrs. Allan Brooks	76	5,150	16	Raining. 2 Common Redpoll (last certain V.I. record 1894). Barn Owl, Audubon's Warbler, Long-billed March Wren.
Vancouver: Vancr. N. H. Society	134	72,500 (abt)	146	Raining. Little Gull, Sora Rail, Anna's Hummingbird. Starling roost not counted therefore total numbers greatly down.
Ladner: Vancouver N.H.S. group	118	103,270	37	Rain/cloudy. Gyrfalcon, 5 Harris' Sparrow. Songbirds down in numbers. Numerous were some ducks, Black-b. Plover, Aud. Warbler, etc.
White Rock: Local group	84	36,431	28	Rainy/windy. Fields flooded, Albino Red-tailed Hawk, Hutton's Vireo, 5 Aud. Warblers, Black-billed Magpie, a possible escape.
Pitt Meadows: Alouette Fld. Natrlsts.	69	—	17	Hutton's Vireo, Harris' Sparrow, 25 Audubon's Warblers, Black-billed Magpie. Out of period: Tr. Swans, Great H. Owl.
Chilliwack: Chwk Field Naturalists	58	3,480	8	Rain/snow. Part albino Oregon Junco, 18 Bald Eagles, 5 Gray-crowned Rosy Finches, Clark's Nutcracker, 59 Whis. Swan.
Kamloops: Kamloops Naturalist Club	32	1,476	21	Part sunny, 4" snow. Half day only — 75 Wh. Swan seen later not included 75 Gray-crowned Rosy Finch,12 Pine Grosbeak.
Salmon Arm: Shuswap Naturalists Club	54	2,470	22	Harris' Sparrow, Golden-crowned Sparrow, 454 Canada Goose.

Vernon: North Okan. Naturalists Club	74	4,745	35	No snow, cloudy. Some species scarce but 321 Canada Geese, 10 Marsh Hawk, 216 Blk-capped Chickadee, 357 Starling, a new high
Kelowna: Central Okan. Natrlsts. Club	72	5,186	20	Cloudy, a little snow. White-throated Sparrow, Harris Sparrow, 65 Ring-billed Gull.
Penticton: South Okan. natrlsts. club	77	10,262	44	Little snow — the day nice. Hawk Owl, White-winged Scoter, White-fronted Goose-stayed with Canadas for 3 weeks.
West Kootenay: West Ktny. Natrlsts. Assn.	66	5,456	72	11 areas total. Gadwall, 395 Mallard, 829 Coot, 399 Black-capped Chickadee, Harris Sparrow, Rufous-sided Towhee.
Williams Lake: Wms. L. Fld. Naturalists	34	510	24	Sunny, 6" snow, lakes frozen. Total numbers down. Few Crows and Redpolls, many Ravens. 1 Chestnut-backed Chickadee.

ALBERTA, SASKATCHEWAN AND MANITOBA

Calgary, Alta.	35	10,198	34	sunny, temp 9-24, snow cover
Edmonton, Alta.	36	3,835	33	sunny, temp 5-8, snow cover
Black Lake, Sask.	4	15	1	light snow, temp 20-9
Harris, Sask.	24	3,353	15	clear, temp 12-18, snow cover, water frozen
Saskatoon, Sask.	28	5,483	32	overcast, temp 20-34, snow cover
Dauplin, Man.	18	1,970	17	high clouds, temp 7-19, water frozen
Oak Lake, Man.	21	1,035	1	overcast, temp 9-0, snow in woods
Pinawa, Man.	19	683	15	temp 2-21, very little open water

ONTARIO AND QUEBEC

Grenville-Hawkesbury	38	1716	14	clear, 25°-25°, calm wind
Hudson, Que.	29	2511	28	snowstorm, 5°-10°, visibility poor
Hull-Ottawa, Que., Ont.	68	11,709	82	clear, -4°-13°, snow cover
Lac Rouillard, Que.	7	63	5	light clouds, -15°-5°, lakes frozen
Lennoxville, Que.	32	2,976	24	lakes frozen, rivers open, 26°-37°
Low, Que.	27	406	2	overcast, 30°-33°, snow cover
Montreal, Que.	32	3,998	29	cloudy AM, clear PM, 0°-3°
Quebec, Que.	36	3,020	23	36 in., snow cover, 16°-25°
Trois-Rivieres, Que.	22	872	25	cloudy AM, 20°-30°, clear PM, calm
Bancroft, Ont.	14	257	2	clear AM, cloudy PM, 15°-26°
Barrie, Ont.	45	2,656	9	overcast and foggy, 32°-42°
Belleville, Ont.	24	1,468	10	cloudy, 15°-20°, 8 in. snow cover, river open
Blenheim, Ont.	90	12,457	22	overcast, 32°-24°, light snow
Carleton Place, Ont.	30	1,144	26	snow all day, 5°-16°, lakes frozen
Deep River, Ont.	31	1,215	19	overcast, snow, lakes frozen
Dryden, Ont.	20	605	15	cloudy to sunny, 12°-22°
Guelph, Ont.	43	4,598	30	freezing rain, overcast, 30°-37°

Location	Species	Birds	Counters	Comment
Hamilton, Ont.	87	58,000	23	clear, 7°-22°, snow cover, harbor open
Kettle Point, Ont.	62	5,669	29	overcast, 35°-40°, snow cover
Kingston, Ont.	83	8,875	48	sun AM, overcast PM, snow cover
Kitchener, Ont.	47	5,139	27	fresh snow, rivers open
London, Ont.	72	4,632	24	heavy snow, blowing, 21°-23°
Long Point, Ont.	91	11,873	25	cloudy, 20°-26°, visibility poor
Manitoulin, Ont.	29	1,181	10	clear AM, cloudy PM, 1°-13° snow
Meadford, Ont.	50	3,543	21	snow cover, drifting, 20°-30°
Minden, Ont.	23	776	9	clear, snow cover, -10°-10°
Moscow, Ont.	28	1,972	12	cloudy, 21°-31°, cone crop good
Napanee Falls, Ont.	36	2,820	14	rain, cloudy, 10°-16°
Niagara Falls, Ont.	71	33,669	28	drizzle, light snow, water pools, 34°-36°
Oshawa, Ont.	65	7,650	16	rain, ponds open, 20°-35°
Owen Sound, Ont.	48	3,275	22	rivers in flood, 40°-50°
Peel-Halton Counties	80	10,793	43	sunny, snow cover, 20-25
Peterborough, Ont.	35	2,455	21	clear, windy, ponds frozen
Pickering Township	76	11,502	22	overcast, green patches, 32°-36°
Point Pelee, Ont.	71	3,891	13	light snow, ponds frozen, 40°-43°
Port Hope-Cobourg	49	4,191	18	snow, lake open, 20°-30°
Presqu'ile Prov. Park	48	3,818	15	variable snow cover, 30°-35°
Richmond Hill, Ont.	50	4,818	44	freezing rain, overcast, 24°-34°
St. Thomas, Ont.	73	11,949	15	cloudy, snow cover, 30°-35°
Sault St. Marie, Ont.	33	972	26	cloudy, snow and ice in bay; 0°-15°
Thunder Bay, Ont.	31	4,421	18	snow, water frozen, 5°-19°
Toronto, Ont.	84	17,631	38	wet snow, creeks open
Westport, Ont.	30	1,232	12	overcast, 16°-35°
Wiarton, Ont.	35	1,465	14	rain, lakes frozen, 25°-40°
Woodhouse Township	69	5,608	18	wet and swampy, 29°-33°

ATLANTIC PROVINCES

Location	Species	Birds	Counters	Comment
Bonne Bay, Nfld.	23	623	9	overcast, light snow; temp. -5° to 1° poor cone crop
St. John's, Nfld.	36	7302	18	cloudy, temp. 10°-18°, 10 in. snow, heavy ice.
Terra Nova Nat Park Nfld.	36	663	7	snowflurries, temp. 14°-18°, salt water inlet freezing
Baddeck, N.S.	30	780	9	overcast, temp. 20°, very little open water
Brier Island, N.S.	55	2436	5	cloudy, temp. 15°-30°, patches of snow
Broad Cove, N.S.	65	4092	11	sunny, temp. 10°-20°, high crusty snow, frozen ponds
Cabot Str. N.S., Nfld.	12	701	2	ferry route Port-aux-Basques to Sydney Hbr.
Cape Breton High Nat. Park, N.S.	44	1281	25	overcast, temp. 15°-30°, 3-4 ft. snow, sea calm

Cheticamp, C.B., N.S.	21	686	4	rain, temp. 34°-39°, snow covered harbor
Esbasoni, N.S.	29	412	4	int. sun and cloud, temp. 21°-25°, ponds and lakes frozen
Glace Bay, N.S.	39	2876	7	overcast, light rain, temp. 33-35 snow cover
Halifax, E.	75	5305	31	mostly sunny, temp 15°-25°, light snow cover, frozen water
Halifax, West	77	10,786	32	cloudy, temp. 15°-25°, ground bare, fresh water frozen
Kajimkujik Nat Park, N.S.	23	266	5	overcast, temp. 20°-28°, good cone crop
Kingston, N.S.	43	1294	8	snow cover, salt water open, fresh water frozen
Louisbourg, C.B., N.S.	40	3130	5	overcast, snowflurries, temp 20°-30°, inland water frozen
Margaree, N.S.	21	538	7	snow cover, fresh water frozen, salt water rough, temp. 22°-25°
Port Hood, N.S.	48	1297	2	clear, temp. 32°-34°, cones poor, berries good
St. Peter's, N.S.	30	296	5	clear, temp. 26°-28°, snow over inland water frozen
Salmon River, C.B., N.S.	21	603	6	snow cover, temp. 5°-18°
Hillsborough, P.E.I.	31	3949	14	sunny, temp. 5°-8°, snow cover
P.E.I. Nat. Park	29	3008	7	cloudy, temp. 9°-14°, open sea areas
Cape Tormentine, N.B.	42	1190	9	cloudy-sunny, temp. 15°-20°
Kouchibouguac Nat. Park, N.B.	15	317	2	sunny, temp. 0°-8°
Nackawic, N.B.	19	820	8	light-overcast, temp. -10°-10°
Sackville, N.B.	34	2564	10	light-overcast, temp. 0°-20°, crusted snow, frozen water

REGIONAL
BIRD CHECK LISTS 🍃🍃🍃

BRITISH COLUMBIA 🍃

Symbols used in this list denote degree of abundance only. Total species 387

C = Common in season in suitable habitat. 236 species

U = Uncommon but found over a wide or local area. 62 species

R = Rare. Very local or unlikely to be seen but regular in occurrence. 35 species

A = Accidental. Well out of its normal range. 42 species

I = Introduced. 12 species

C	Common Loon	U	Trumpeter Swan
R	Yellow-billed Loon	C	Canada Goose
C	Arctic Loon	A	Brant
C	Red-throated Loon	C	Black Brant
C	Red-necked Grebe	R	Emperor Goose
C	Horned Grebe	C	White-fronted Goose
C	Eared Grebe	C	Snow Goose
C	Western Grebe	A	Blue Goose
C	Pied-billed Grebe	A	Ross' Goose
A	Short-tailed Albatross	A	Fulvous Tree Duck
C	Black-footed Albatross	C	Mallard
C	Fulmar	C	Gadwall
C	Pink-footed Shearwater	C	Pintail
U	Pale-footed Shearwater	A	Falcated Teal
U	New Zealand Shearwater	A	Common Teal
C	Sooty Shearwater	C	Green-winged Teal
U	Slender-billed Shearwater	A	Baikal Teal
R	Manx Shearwater	C	Blue-winged Teal
U	Fork-tailed Petrel	C	Cinnamon Teal
U	Leach's Petrel	U	European Widgeon
U	White Pelican	C	American Widgeon
A	Brown Pelican	C	Shoveler
C	Double-crested Cormorant	C	Wood Duck
C	Brandt's Cormorant	C	Redhead
C	Pelagic Cormorant	C	Ring-necked Duck
C	Great Blue Heron	C	Canvasback

110

U	Green Heron	C	Greater Scaup
A	Snowy Egret	C	Lesser Scaup
A	Black-crowned Night Heron	A	Tufted Duck
R	American Bittern	C	Common Goldeneye
I	Mute Swan	C	Barrow's Goldeneye
C	Whistling Swan	C	Bufflehead
C	Oldsquaw	U	American Golden Plover
C	Harlequin Duck	C	Black-bellied Plover
A	Steller's Eider	C	Surfbird
A	Common Eider	C	Ruddy Turnstone
A	King Eider	C	Black Turnstone
A	Spectacled Eider	C	Common Snipe
C	White-winged Scoter	U	Long-billed Curlew
C	Surf Scoter	U	Whimbrel
C	Common Scoter	R	Upland Plover
C	Ruddy Duck	C	Spotted Sandpiper
U	Hooded Merganser	C	Solitary Sandpiper
C	Common Merganser	C	Wandering Tattler
C	Red-breasted Merganser	A	Willet
U	Turkey Vulture	C	Greater Yellowlegs
U	Goshawk	C	Lesser Yellowlegs
C	Sharp-shinned Hawk	R	Knot
C	Cooper Hawk	C	Rock Sandpiper
C	Red-tailed Hawk	A	Sharp-tailed Sandpiper
R	Harlan's Hawk	C	Pectoral Sandpiper
U	Swainson's Hawk	A	White-rumped Sandpiper
U	Rough-legged Hawk	C	Baird's Sandpiper
U	Golden Eagle	C	Least Sandpiper
C	Bald Eagle	A	Curlew Sandpiper
C	Marsh Hawk	C	Dunlin
U	Osprey	C	Short-billed Dowitcher
R	Gyr Falcon	C	Long-billed Dowitcher
R	Prairie Falcon	U	Stilt Sandpiper
R	Peregrine Falcon	U	Semi-palmated Sandpiper
U	Pigeon Hawk	C	Western Sandpiper
C	Sparrow Hawk	R	Buff-breasted Sandpiper
C	Blue Grouse	R	Marbled Godwit
C	Spruce Grouse	A	Bar-tailed Godwit
C	Ruffed Grouse	R	Hudsonian Godwit
C	Willow Ptarmigan	C	Sanderling
C	Rock Ptarmigan	R	Avocet
C	White-tailed Ptarmigan	C	Red Phalarope
R	Sharp-tailed Grouse	C	Wilson's Phalarope
A	Sage Grouse	C	Northern Phalarope
I	Bobwhite	R	Pomarine Jaeger
I	California Quail	C	Parasitic Jaeger
I	Mountain Quail	U	Long-tailed Jaeger
I	Ring-necked Pheasant	A	Skua
I	Chukar	R	Glaucous Gull
I	Gray Partridge	C	Glaucous-winged Gull
U	Sandhill Crane	R	Western Gull
U	Virginia Rail	C	Herring Gull
C	Sora	C	California Gull
C	American Coot	C	Ring-billed Gull
C	Black Oystercatcher	C	Mew Gull
C	Semi-palmated Plover	U	Franklin's Gull
C	Killdeer	C	Bonaparte's Gull

C	Heermann's Gull		C	Downy Woodpecker
A	Ivory Gull		R	White-headed Woodpecker
C	Black-legged Kittiwake		U	Black-backed Three-toed Woodpecker
A	Ross' Gull			
C	Sabine's Gull		U	Northern Three-toed Wood-pecker
A	Forester's Tern			
C	Common Tern		C	Eastern Kingbird
C	Arctic Tern		A	Gray Kingbird
U	Caspian Tern		A	Tropical Kingbird
C	Black Tern		C	Western Kingbird
C	Common Murre		A	Scissor-tailed Flycatcher
A	Thick-billed Murre		A	Ash-throated Flycatcher
C	Pigeon Guillemot		U	Eastern Phoebe
C	Marbled Murrelet		A	Black Phoebe
C	Ancient Murrelet		U	Say's Phoebe
U	Cassin's Auklet		U	Yellow-bellied Flycatcher
C	Rhinoceros Auklet		A	Acadian Flycatcher
C	Tufted Puffin		C	Traill's Flycatcher
C	Band-tailed Pigeon		C	Least Flycatcher
I	Rock Dove		C	Hammond's Flycatcher
A	White-winged Dove		C	Dusky Flycatcher
C	Mourning Dove		C	Western Flycatcher
A	Yellow-billed Cuckoo		C	Western Wood Pewee
R	Barn Owl		C	Olive-sided Flycatcher
C	Screech Owl		I	Skylark
A	Flammulated Owl		C	Horned Lark
U	Great Horned Owl		C	Violet-green Swallow
U	Snowy Owl		C	Tree Swallow
R	Hawk Owl		C	Bank Swallow
U	Pygmy Owl		C	Rough-winged Swallow
R	Burrowing Owl		C	Barn Swallow
U	Barred Owl		C	Cliff Swallow
R	Spotted Owl		R	Purple Martin
R	Great Gray Owl		C	Gray Jay
U	Long-eared Owl		A	Blue Jay
C	Short-eared Owl		C	Steller's Jay
R	Boreal Owl		C	Black-billed Magpie
R	Saw-whet Owl		C	Common Raven
U	Poorwill		C	Common Crow
C	Common Nighthawk		C	Northwestern Crow
C	Black Swift		C	Clark's Nutcracker
C	Vaux Swift		C	Black-capped Chickadee
U	White-throated Swift		C	Mountain Chickadee
C	Black-chinned Hummingbird		U	Boreal Chickadee
U	Anna's Hummingbird		C	Chestnut-backed Chickadee
C	Rufous Hummingbird		C	Common Bushtit
C	Calliope Hummingbird		C	White-breasted Nuthatch
C	Belted Kingfisher		C	Red-breasted Nuthatch
C	Yellow-shafted Flicker		C	Pygmy Nuthatch
C	Red-shafted Flicker		C	Brown Creeper
U	Pileated Woodpecker		C	American Dipper
A	Red-headed Woodpecker		C	House Wren
C	Lewis' Woodpecker		C	Winter Wren
C	Yellow-bellied Sapsucker		C	Bewick's Wren
R	Williamson's Sapsucker		C	Long-billed Marsh Wren
C	Hairy Woodpecker		R	Canyon Wren

112

U	Rock Wren
A	Mockingbird
C	Catbird
R	Sage Thrasher
C	American Robin
C	Varied Thrush
C	Hermit Thrush
C	Swainson's Thrush
U	Gray-cheeked Thrush
C	Veery
U	Western Bluebird
C	Mountain Bluebird
U	Townsend's Solitaire
A	Blue-gray Gnatcatcher
C	Golden-crowned Kinglet
C	Ruby-crowned Kinglet
C	Water Pipit
C	Bohemian Waxwing
C	Cedar Waxwing
C	Northern Shrike
A	Loggerhead Shrike
I	Starling
I	Crested Mynah
U	Hutton's Vireo
C	Solitary Vireo
C	Red-eyed Vireo
U	Philadelphia Vireo
C	Warbling Vireo
U	Black-and-white Warbler
C	Tennessee Warbler
C	Orange-crowned Warbler
U	Nashville Warbler
C	Yellow Warbler
C	Magnolia Warbler
R	Cape May Warbler
C	Myrtle Warbler
C	Audubon's Warbler
C	Black-throated Gray Warbler
C	Townsend's Warbler
A	Black-throated Green Warbler
R	Bay-breasted Warbler
C	Blackpoll Warbler
U	Palm Warbler
C	Ovenbird
C	Northern Waterthrush
U	Connecticut Warbler
C	Macgillivray's Warbler
C	Yellowthroat
U	Yellow-breasted Chat
C	Wilson's Warbler
C	American Redstart
I	House Sparrow
U	Bobolink
C	Western Meadowlark
C	Yellow-headed Blackbird

C	Red-winged Blackbird
R	Baltimore Oriole
C	Bullock's Oriole
C	Rusty Blackbird
C	Brewer's Blackbird
C	Common Grackle
C	Brown-headed Cowbird
C	Western Tanager
A	Scarlet Tanager
C	Rose-breasted Grosbeak
C	Black-headed Grosbeak
A	Indigo Bunting
C	Lazuli Bunting
A	Dickcissel
C	Evening Grosbeak
C	Purple Finch
C	Cassin's Finch
C	House Finch
C	Pine Grosbeak
U	Gray-crowned Rosy Finch
U	Hoary Redpoll
C	Common Redpoll
C	Pine Siskin
C	American Goldfinch
A	Lesser Goldfinch
C	Red Crossbill
C	White-winged Crossbill
C	Rufous-sided Towhee
A	Lark Bunting
C	Savannah Sparrow
R	Grasshopper Sparrow
U	Leconte's Sparrow
U	Sharp-tailed Sparrow
C	Vesper Sparrow
C	Lark Sparrow
A	Black-throated Sparrow
A	Sage Sparrow
C	Slate-colored Junco
C	Oregon Junco
C	Tree Sparrow
C	Chipping Sparrow
U	Clay-colored Sparrow
C	Brewer's Sparrow
R	Harris' Sparrow
C	White-crowned Sparrow
C	Golden-crowned Sparrow
C	White-throated Sparrow
C	Fox Sparrow
C	Lincoln's Sparrow
C	Swamp Sparrow
C	Song Sparrow
A	McCown's Longspur
U	Lapland Longspur
A	Smith's Longspur
A	Chestnut-collared Longspur
U	Snow Bunting

ALBERTA, SASKATCHEWAN
AND MANITOBA

Common Loon
Yellow-billed Loon
Arctic Loon
Red-throated Loon
Red-necked Grebe
Horned Grebe
Eared Grebe
Western Grebe
Pied-billed Grebe
White Pelican
Double-crested Cormorant
Great Blue Heron
Green Heron
Little Blue Heron
Cattle Egret
Common Egret
Snowy Egret
Black-crowned Night Heron
Least Bittern
American Bittern
Mute Swan
Whistling Swan
Trumpeter Swan
Canada Goose
Brant
    (incl. Black Brant)

Gadwall
Pintail
Green-winged Teal
Blue-winged Teal
Cinnamon Teal
European Widgeon
American Widgeon
Shoveler
Wood Duck
Redhead
Ring-necked Duck
Canvasback
Greater Scaup
Lesser Scaup
Common Goldeneye
Barrow's Goldeneye
Bufflehead
Oldsqaw
Harlequin Duck
Common Eider
King Eider
White-winged Scoter
Surf Scoter
Common Scoter
Ruddy Duck
Hooded Merganser

White-fronted Goose
Snow Goose
  (incl. Blue Goose)
Ross's Goose
Mallard
Black Duck
Cooper's Hawk
Red-tailed Hawk
  (incl. Harlan's Hawk)
Broad-winged Hawk
Swainson's Hawk
Rough-legged Hawk
Ferruginous Hawk
Golden Eagle
Bald Eagle
Marsh Hawk
Osprey
Gyrfalcon
Prairie Falcon
Peregrine Falcon
Pigeon Hawk
Sparrow Hawk
Blue Grouse
Spruce Grouse
Willow Ptarmigan
Rock Ptarmigan
White-tailed Ptarmigan
Greater Prairie Chicken
Sharp-tailed Grouse
Sage Grouse
Ring-necked Pheasant
Chukar
Gray Partridge
Whooping Crane
Sandhill Crane
Common Crane
King Rail
Virginia Rail
Sora
Yellow Rail
American Coot
Semipalmated Plover
Piping Plover
Snowy Plover
Killdeer
Mountain Plover
Surfbird
Ruddy Turnstone
Black Turnstone
American Woodcock
Common Snipe
Long-billed Curlew
Whimbrel
Eskimo Curlew
Upland Plover
Spotted Sandpiper
Solitary Sandpiper

Common Merganser
Red-breasted Merganser
Turkey Vulture
Black Vulture
Goshawk
Sharp-shinned Hawk
Willet
Greater Yellowlegs
Lesser Yellowlegs
Spotted Redshank
Knot
Pectoral Sandpiper
White-rumped Sandpiper
Baird's Sandpiper
Least Sandpiper
Curlew Sandpiper
Dunlin
Short-billed Dowitcher
Long-billed Dowitcher
Stilt Sandpiper
Semipalmated Sandpiper
Marbled Godwit
Hudsonian Godwit
Ruff
Sanderling
American Avocet
Red Phalarope
Wilson's Phalarope
Northern Phalarope
Pomarine Jaeger
Parasitic Jaeger
Glaucous-winged Gull
Lesser Black-backed Gull
Herring Gull
Thayer's Gull
California Gull
Ring-billed Gull
Mew Gull
Franklin's Gull
Bonaparte's Gull
Little Gull
Forster's Tern
Common Tern
Arctic Tern
Caspian Tern
Black Tern
Rock Dove
Mourning Dove
Yellow-billed Cuckoo
Black-billed Cuckoo
Barn Owl
Screech Owl
Great Horned Owl
Snowy Owl
Hawk Owl
Burrowing Owl
Barred Owl

Spotted Owl
Great Gray Owl
Long-eared Owl
Short-eared Owl
Boreal Owl
Saw-whet Owl
Whip-poor-will
Poor-will
Common Nighthawk
Black Swift
Chimney Swift
Vaux's Swift
Ruby-throated Hummingbird
Calliope Hummingbird
Belted Kingfisher
Yellow-shafted Flicker
Red-shafted Flicker
Pileated Woodpecker
Red-bellied Woodpecker
Red-headed Woodpecker
Lewis's Woodpecker
Yellow-bellied Sapsucker
Hairy Woodpecker
Downy Woodpecker
Black-backed Three-toed
  Woodpecker
Northern Three-toed
  Woodpecker
Eastern Kingbird
Western Kingbird
Great Crested Flycatcher
Eastern Phoebe
Say's Phoebe
Yellow-bellied Flycatcher
Traill's Flycatcher
Least Flycatcher
Hammond's Flycatcher
Dusky Flycatcher
Western Flycatcher
Eastern Wood Pewee
Western Wood Pewee
Olive-sided Flycatcher
Horned Lark
Violet-green Swallow
Tree Swallow
Bank Swallow
Rough-winged Swallow
Barn Swallow
Cliff Swallow
Cave Swallow
Purple Martin
Gray Jay
Blue Jay
Steller's Jay
Black-billed Magpie
Common Raven

Common Crow
Clark's Nutcracker
Black-capped Chickadee
Mountain Chickadee
Boreal Chickadee
White-breasted Nuthatch
Red-breasted Nuthatch
Brown Creeper
House Wren
Winter Wren
Long-billed Marsh Wren
Short-billed Marsh Wren
Rock Wren
Northern Mockingbird
Catbird
Brown Thrasher
Sage Thrasher
American Robin
Varied Thrush
Hermit Thrush
Swainson's Thrush
Grey-cheeked Thrush
Veery
Eastern Bluebird
Western Bluebird
Mountain Bluebird
Golden-crowned Kinglet
Ruby-crowned Kinglet
Water Pipit
Sprague's Pipit
Bohemian Waxwing
Cedar Waxwing
Northern Shrike
Loggerhead Shrike
Common Starling
Solitary Vireo
Red-eyed Vireo
Philadelphia Vireo
Warbling Vireo
Black-and-white Warbler
Tennessee Warbler
Orange-crowned Warbler
Nashville Warbler
Parula Warbler
Yellow Warbler
Magnolia Warbler
Cape May Warbler
Myrtle Warbler
Audubon's Warbler
Townsend's Warbler
Black-throated Green
  Warbler
Cerulean Warbler
Blackburnian Warbler
Chestnut-sided Warbler
Bay-breasted Warbler

116

Blackpoll Warbler
Prairie Warbler
Palm Warbler
Ovenbird
Northern Waterthrush
Connecticut Warbler
Mourning Warbler
MacGillvray's Warbler
Common Yellowthroat
Yellow-breasted Chat
Wilson's Warbler
Canada Warbler
American Redstart
House Sparrow
Bobolink
Western Meadowlark
Yellow-headed Blackbird
Red-winged Blackbird
Orchard Oriole
Baltimore Oriole
Bullock's Oriole
Rusty Blackbird
Brewer's Blackbird
Common Grackle
Brown-headed Cowbird
Western Tanager
Scarlet Tanager
Cardinal
Rose-breasted Grosbeak
Black-headed Grosbeak
Indigo Bunting
Lazuli Bunting
Dickcissel
Evening Grosbeak

Purple Finch
Cassin's Finch
Pine Grosbeak
Common Redpoll
Pine Siskin
American Goldfinch
Red Crossbill
White-winged Crossbill
Rufous-sided Towhee
Lark Bunting
Savannah Sparrow
Baird's Sparrow
Le Conte's Sparrow
Sharp-tailed Sparrow
Vesper Sparrow
Lark Sparrow
Slate-colored Junco
Tree Sparrow
Chipping Sparrow
Clay-colored Sparrow
Brewer's Sparrow
White-crowned Sparrow
Golden-crowned Sparrow
White-throated Sparrow
Fox Sparrow
Lincoln's Sparrow
Swamp Sparrow
Song Sparrow
McCown's Longspur
Lapland Longspur
Smith's Longspur
Chestnut-collared
  Longspur
Snow Bunting.

ONTARIO AND QUEBEC

Common Loon
Arctic Loon
Red-throated Loon
Red-necked Grebe
Horned Grebe
Western Grebe
Pied-billed Grebe
Yellow-nosed Albatross
Northern Fulmar
Greater Shearwater
Sooty Shearwater
Black-capped Petrel
Leach's Petrel
Harcourt's Petrel
Wilson's Petrel
White Pelican
Gannet
Great Cormorant
Double-crested Cormorant
Anhinga
Magnificent Frigatebird
Great Blue Heron
Green Heron
Little Blue Heron
Cattle Egret
Common Egret

Wood Ibis
Glossy Ibis
White Ibis
Mute Swan
Whistling Swan
Trumpeter Swan
Canada Goose
Brant
   (incl. Black Brant)
Barnacle Goose
White-fronted Goose
Snow Goose
   (incl. Blue Goose)
Ross's Goose
Fulvous Tree Duck
Mallard
Black Duck
Gadwall
Pintail
Green-winged Teal
Blue-winged Teal
Cinnamon Teal
European Widgeon
American Widgeon
Shoveler
Wood Duck

Snowy Egret
Louisiana Heron
Black-crowned Night Heron
Yellow-crowned Night Heron
Least Bittern
American Bittern
Barrow's Goldeneye
Bufflehead
Oldsqaw
Harlequin Duck
Steller's Eider
Common Eider
King Eider
White-winged Scoter
Surf Scoter
Common Scoter
Ruddy Duck
Hooded Merganser
Common Merganser
Red-breasted Merganser
Smew
Turkey Vulture
Black Vulture
Swallow-tailed Kite
Goshawk
Sharp-shinned Hawk
Cooper's Hawk
Red-tailed Hawk
  (incl. Harlan's Hawk)
Red-shouldered Hawk
Broad-winged Hawk
Swainson's Hawk
Rough-legged Hawk
Ferruginous Hawk
Golden Eagle
Bald Eagle
Marsh Hawk
Osprey
Crested Caracara
Gyrfalcon
Peregrine Falcon
Pigeon Hawk
Sparrow Hawk
Spruce Grouse
Ruffed Grouse
Willow Ptarmigan
Rock Ptarmigan
Greater Prairie Chicken
Sharp-tailed Grouse
Bobwhite
Ring-necked Pheasant
Gray Partridge
Turkey
Whooping Crane
Sandhill Crane
King Rail
Virginia Rail

Redhead
Ring-necked Duck
Canvasback
Greater Scaup
Lesser Scaup
Common Goldeneye
Sora
Yellow Rail
Purple Gallinule
Common Gallinule
American Coot
American Oystercatcher
Lapwing
Semipalmated Plover
Piping Plover
Snowy Plover
Killdeer
Ruddy Turnstone
American Woodcock
Common Snipe
Long-billed Curlew
Whimbrel
Eskimo Curlew
Upland Plover
Spotted Sandpiper
Solitary Sandpiper
Willet
Greater Yellowlegs
Lesser Yellowlegs
Knot
Purple Sandpiper
Pectoral Sandpiper
White-rumped Sandpiper
Baird's Sandpiper
Least Sandpiper
Curlew Sandpiper
Dunlin
Short-billed Dowitcher
Long-billed Dowitcher
Stilt Sandpiper
Semipalmated Sandpiper
Western Sandpiper
Buff-breasted Sandpiper
Marbled Godwit
Hudsonian Godwit
Ruff
Sanderling
American Avocet
Red Phalarope
Wilson's Phalarope
Northern Phalarope
Pomarine Jaeger
Parasitic Jaeger
Glaucous Gull
Iceland Gull
Great Black-backed Gull
Herring Gull

Ring-billed Gull
Black-headed Gull
Laughing Gull
Franklin's Gull
Bonaparte's Gull
Little Gull
Black-legged Kittiwake
Forster's Tern
Common Tern
Arctic Tern
Caspian Tern
Black Tern
Razorbill
Common Murre
Thick-billed Murre
Dovekie
Black Guillemot
Ancient Murrelet
Common Puffin
Rock Dove
Mourning Dove
Yellow-billed Cuckoo
Black-billed Cuckoo
Barn Owl
Great Horned Owl
Snowy Owl
Hawk Owl
Burrowing Owl
Barred Owl
Spotted Owl
Great Gray Owl
Short-eared Owl
Boreal Owl
Saw-whet Owl
Chuck-will's-widow
Whip-poor-will
Common Nighthawk
Black Swift
Chimney Swift
Ruby-throated Hummingbird
Belted Kingfisher
Yellow-shafted Flicker
Pileated Woodpecker
Red-bellied Woodpecker
Red-headed Woodpecker
Lewis's Woodpecker
Yellow-bellied Sapsucker
Black-backed Three-toed
  Woodpecker
Northern Three-toed
  Woodpecker
Eastern Kingbird
Western Kingbird
Great Crested Flycatcher
Eastern Phoebe
Yellow-bellied Flycatcher
Acadian Flycatcher

Traill's Flycatcher
Least Flycatcher
Eastern Wood Pewee
Olive-sided Flycatcher
Horned Lark
Tree Swallow
Bank Swallow
Rough-winged Swallow
Barn Swallow
Cliff Swallow
Cave Swallow
Purple Martin
Gray Jay
Blue Jay
Steller's Jay
Black-billed Magpie
Common Raven
Common Crow
Black-capped Chickadee
Tufted Titmouse
White-breasted Nuthatch
Red-breasted Nuthatch
Brown Creeper
House Wren
Winter Wren
Bewick's Wren
Carolina Wren
Long-billed Marsh Wren
Short-billed Marsh Wren
Northern Mockingbird
Catbird
Brown Thrasher
American Robin
Varied Thrush
Wood Thrush
Hermit Thrush
Swainson's Thrush
Gray-cheeked Thrush
Veery
Eastern Bluebird
Mountain Bluebird
Wheatear
Blue-gray Gnatcatcher
Golden-crowned Kinglet
Ruby-crowned Kinglet
Water Pipit
Cedar Waxwing
Northern Shrike
Loggerhead Shrike
Common Starling
White-eyed Vireo
Yellow-throated Vireo
Solitary Vireo
Red-eyed Vireo
Philadelphia Vireo
Warbling Vireo
Black-and-white Warbler

Prothonotary Warbler
Golden-winged warbler
Blue-winged Warbler
Tennessee Warbler
Nashville Warbler
Parula Warbler
Yellow Warbler
Magnolia Warbler
Cape May Warbler
Black-throated Blue
 Warbler
Myrtle Warbler
Black-throated Green
 Warbler
Cerulean Warbler
Blackburnian Warbler
Chestnut-sided Warbler
Bay-breasted Warbler
Blackpoll Warbler
Pine Warbler
Kirtland's Warbler
Prairie Warbler
Palm Warbler
Ovenbird
Northern Waterthrush
Louisiana Waterthrush
Connecticut Warbler
Mourning Warbler
Common Yellowthroat
Hooded Warbler
Wilson's Warbler
Canada Warbler
American Redstart
House Sparrow
Bobolink
Eastern Meadowlark
Western Madowlark
Yellow-headed blackbird
Red-winged Blackbird
Orchard Oriole
Baltimore Oriole

Rusty Blackbird
Brewer's Blackbird
Common Grackle
Brown-headed Cowbird
Western Tanager
Scarlet Tanager
Summer Tanager
Cardinal
Rose-breasted Grosbeak
Blue Grosbeak
Indigo Bunting
Evening Grosbeak
Purple Finch
Pine Grosbeak
Common Redpoll
Pine Siskin
American Goldfinch
Red Crossbill
White-winged Crossbill
Rufous-sided Towhee
Savannah Sparrow
Grasshopper Sparrow
Le Conte's Sparrow
Henslow's Sparrow
Sharp-tailed Sparrow
Vesper Sparrow
Lark Sparrow
Slate-colored Junco
Tree Sparrow
Chipping Sparrow
Clay-colored Sparrow
Field Sparrow
Harris's Sparrow
White-crowned Sparrow
White-throated Sparrow
Fox Sparrow
Lincoln's Sparrow
Swamp Sparrow
Song Sparrow
Lapland Longspur
Snow Bunting

ATLANTIC PROVINCES

Common Loon
Red-throated Loon
Red-necked Grebe
Horned Grebe
Pied-billed Grebe
Yellow-nosed Albatross
Northern Fulmar
Cory's Shearwater
Greater Shearwater
Sooty Shearwater
Manx Shearwater
Little Shearwater
Black-capped Petrel
Leach's Petrel
Wilson's Petrel
White-tailed Tropicbird
White Pelican
Brown Pelican
Brown Booby
Gannet
Great Cormorant
Double-crested Cormorant
Magnificent Frigatebird
Great Blue Heron
Green Heron
Little Blue Heron

Yellow-crowned Night Heron
Least Bittern
American Bittern
Wood Ibis
Glossy Ibis
White Ibis
Mute Swan
Whistling Swan
Canada Goose
Brant
   (incl. Black Brant)
White-fronted Goose
   (incl. Blue Goose)
Fulvous Tree Duck
Mallard
Black Duck
Gadwall
Pintail
Common Teal
Green-winged Teal
Blue-winged Teal
European Widgeon
American Widgeon
Shoveler
Wood Duck
Redhead

Cattle Egret
Common Egret
Snowy Egret
Little Egret
Louisiana Heron
Black-crowned Night Heron
Bufflehead
Oldsquaw
Harlequin Duck
Common Eider
King Eider
White-winged Scoter
Surf Scoter
Common Scoter
Ruddy Duck
Hooded Merganser
Common Merganser
Red-breasted Merganser
Turkey Vulture
Black Vulture
Goshawk
Sharp-shinned Hawk
Cooper's Hawk
Red-tailed Hawk
    (incl. Harlan's Hawk)
Red-shouldered Hawk
Broad-winged Hawk
Rough-legged Hawk
Golden Eagle
Bald Eagle
Marsh Hawk
Osprey
Gyrfalcon
Peregrine Falcon
Pigeon Hawk
Sparrow Hawk
Spruce Grouse
Ruffed Grouse
Willow Ptarmigan
Rock Ptarmigan
Ring-necked Pheasant
Gray Partridge
Sandhill Crane
King Rail
Clapper Rail
Virginia Rail
Sora
Yellow Rail
Corn Crake
Purple Gallinule
Common Gallinule
European Coot
American Coot
American Oystercatcher
Lapwing
Semipalmated Plover
Piping Plover

Ring-necked Duck
Canvasback
Greater Scaup
Lesser Scaup
Common Goldeneye
Barrow's Goldeneye
Snowy Plover
Wilson's Plover
Killdeer
Eurasian Golden Plover
Ruddy Turnstone
American Woodcock
Common Snipe
Long-billed Curlew
Whimbrel
Eskimo Curlew
Upland Plover
Spotted Sandpiper
Solitary Sandpiper
Willet
Greater Yellowlegs
Lesser Yellowlegs
Spotted Redshank
Knot
Purple Sandpiper
Pectoral Sandpiper
White-rumped Sandpiper
Baird's Sandpiper
Least Sandpiper
Curlew Sandpiper
Dunlin
Short-billed Dowitcher
Long-billed Dowitcher
Stilt Sandpiper
Semipalmated Sandpiper
Buff-breasted Sandpiper
Marbled Godwit
Hudsonian Godwit
Black-tailed Godwit
Ruff
Sanderling
American Avocet
Wilson's Phalarope
Northern Phalarope
Parasitic Jaeger
Skua
Glaucous Gull
Iceland Gull
Great Black-backed Gull
Herring Gull
Ring-billed Gull
Black-headed Gull
Laughing Gull
Bonaparte's Gull
Little Gull
Black-legged Kittiwake
Common Tern

Arctic Tern	Barn Swallow
Roseate Tern	Cliff Swallow
Caspian Tern	Cave Swallow
Black Tern	Purple Martin
Black Skimmer	Gray Jay
Razorbill	Blue Jay
Common Murre	Steller's Jay
Thick-billed Murre	Common Raven
Dovekie	Common Crow
Black Guillemot	Black-capped Chickadee
Ancient Murrelet	White-breasted Nuthatch
Common Puffin	Red-breasted Nuthatch
Rock Dove	Brown Creeper
Mourning Dove	House Wren
Yellow-billed Cuckoo	Winter Wren
Black-billed Cuckoo	Long-billed Marsh Wren
Barn Owl	Short-billed Marsh Wren
Great Horned Owl	Northern Mockingbird
Snowy Owl	Catbird
Hawk Owl	Brown Thrasher
Barred Owl	American Robin
Great Gray Owl	Varied Thrush
Long-eared Owl	Hermit Thrush
Short-eared Owl	Swainson's Thrush
Boreal Owl	Grey-cheeked Thrush
Saw-whet Owl	Veery
Chuck-will's-widow	Eastern Bluebird
Whip-poor-will	Wheatear
Common Nighthawk	Blue-gray Gnatcatcher
Chimney Swift	Golden-crowned Kinglet
Ruby-throated Hummingbird	Ruby-crowned Kinglet
Belted Kingfisher	Water Pipit
Yellow-shafted Flicker	Cedar Waxwing
Red-shafted Flicker	Northern Shrike
Pileated Woodpecker	Loggerhead Shrike
Red-bellied Woodpecker	Common Starling
Red-headed Woodpecker	Yellow-throated Vireo
Yellow-bellied Sapsucker	Solitary Vireo
Black-backed Three-toed Woodpecker	Red-eyed Vireo
	Philadelphia Vireo
Northern Three-toed Woodpecker	Warbling Vireo
	Black-and-white Warbler
Eastern Kingbird	Tennessee Warbler
Western Kingbird	Orange-crowned Warbler
Great Crested Flycatcher	Nashville Warbler
Eastern Phoebe	Parula Warbler
Yellow-bellied Flycatcher	Yellow Warbler
Traill's Flycatcher	Magnolia Warbler
Least Flycatcher	Cape May Warbler
Eastern Wood Pewee	Black-throated Blue Warbler
Olive-sided Flycatcher	
Horned Lark	Myrtle Warbler
Violet-green Swallow	Black-throated Green Warbler
Tree Swallow	
Bank Swallow	Blackburnian Warbler
Rough-winged Swallow	Chestnut-sided Warbler

Bay-breasted Warbler
Blackpoll Warbler
Palm Warbler
Ovenbird
Northern Waterthrush
Louisiana Waterthrush
Connecticut Warbler
Mourning Warbler
Common Yellowthroat
Wilson's Warbler
Canada Warbler
American Redstart
House Sparrow
Bobolink
Eastern Meadowlark
Western Meadowlark
Red-winged Blackbird
Baltimore Oriole
Rusty Blackbird
Brewer's Blackbird
Common Grackle
Brown-headed Cowbird
Western Tanager
Scarlet Tanager
Cardinal
Rose-breasted Grosbeak
Indigo Bunting
Dickcissel
Evening Grosbeak

Purple Finch
Pine Grosbeak
Hoary Redpoll
Common Redpoll
Pine Siskin
American Goldfinch
Red Crossbill
White-winged Crossbill
Rufous-sided Towhee
Ispwich Sparrow
Savannah Sparrow
Grasshopper Sparrow
Le Conte's Sparrow
Sharp-tailed Sparrow
Vesper Sparrow
Lark Sparrow
Slate-colored Junco
Tree Sparrow
Chipping Sparrow
Clay-colored Sparrow
Field Sparrow
White-crowned Sparrow
White-throated Sparrow
Fox Sparrow
Lincoln's Sparrow
Swamp Sparrow
Song Sparrow
Lapland Longspur
Snow Bunting

REFERENCES

General

The Birds of Canada by W. E. Godfrey
Birds of the Eastern Forest (Volume 1)
Birds of the Eastern Forest (Volume 2)
Birds of the Northern Forest
  by Lansdowne & Livingston
A Field Guide to the Birds by Peterson
Birds of North America by Robbins et al
Ducks, Geese and Swans of North America
  by Kortwright

Birds of Canada Series by David Hancock, Jim Woodford
and David Stirling. four regional Canadian editions:
1) Atlantic Provinces 2) Ontario and Quebec 3) Alberta,
Saskatchewan and Manitoba, and 4) British Columbia.

Atlantic Provinces

The Birds of New Brunswick by W. Austin Squires
A Naturalist in New Brunswick by W. Austin Squires
The Bird Life of Grand Manan Archipelago by O. S. Pettingill
Birds of Newfoundland by Harold S. Peters and
  T. D. Burleigh
Birds of Nova Scotia by Robie W. Tufts
Birds of Cape Breton by W. E. Godfrey

Ontario and Quebec

Breeding Birds of Ontario by James L. Baillie
  and Paul Harrington. (out of print but available
  in libraries)
Birds of Simcoe County by O. E. Devitt
History of the Birds of Kingston by Helen R. Quilliam
Ontario Birds by L. L. Snyder
Oiseaux du Quebec by Jean Bedard
Birds of the Labrador Peninsula and Adjacent Areas
  by W. E. C. Todd
Birds of the Ungava Peninsula by Francis Harper

Alberta, Saskatchewan and Manitoba

The Birds of Alberta by W. Ray Salt
and A. L. Wilk
Alberta: A Natural History by W. G. Hardy
Birds of Jasper National Park by I. McT. Cowan,
Canadian Wildlife Service, 1955.
Birds of Regina by Margaret Belcher, Sask. Natural
History Soc. 1961
Birds of the Cypress Hills and Flotten Lake Regions
by W. E. Godfrey, National Museum of Canada Bull.
120, 1950.
The Birds of Prince Albert National Park by J.D. Soper
Canada Wildlife Service Bull. 2 1952.

British Columbia

In addition to the check lists prepared by many of British
Columbia's natural history societies and the two major monthly
publications, *Discovery* and *The Victoria Naturalist*, the following literature is recommended reading for birdwatchers:

Hancock's Ferry Guide to Vancouver Island, by David Hancock

A Review of the Bird Fauna of British Columbia, by J. A.
Munro and I. McT. Cowan. (This is a scientific catalogue now
out of print but available in many libraries.)

Provincial Museum Handbooks, each book dealing with one or
more bird families.

Annotated List of the Birds of Southern Vancouver Island:
by A. R. Davidson

The Birds of Vancouver Island: (an annotated list), by David
Stirling

Vancouver's Birds: by John Rogers

Vancouver Birds in 1971: edited by R. Wayne Campbell et al.

Annual Bird Report (Victoria) 1971, edited by Dr. J. B. Tatum,
Victoria

Birds of the Early Explorers in the Northern Pacific, by
Theed Pearse, 275 pp.

Litho by D. W. Friesen & Sons Ltd., Altona, Manitoba, Canada